GENESIS

By Stephen Mitchell

POETRY
Parables and Portraits

PROSE
The Gospel According to Jesus

TRANSLATIONS AND ADAPTATIONS
Genesis: A New Translation of the Classic Biblical Stories
Ahead of All Parting: The Selected Poetry and Prose of Rainer Maria Rilke
A Book of Psalms
The Selected Poetry of Dan Pagis
Tao Te Ching
The Book of Job
The Selected Poetry of Yehuda Amichai *(with Chana Bloch)*
The Sonnets to Orpheus
The Lay of the Love and Death of Cornet Christoph Rilke
Letters to a Young Poet
The Notebooks of Malte Laurids Brigge
The Selected Poetry of Rainer Maria Rilke

EDITED BY STEPHEN MITCHELL
Song of Myself
Into the Garden: A Wedding Anthology *(with Robert Hass)*
The Enlightened Mind: An Anthology of Sacred Prose
The Enlightened Heart: An Anthology of Sacred Poetry
Dropping Ashes on the Buddha: The Teaching of Zen Master Seung Sahn

FOR CHILDREN
The Creation *(with paintings by Ori Sherman)*

BOOKS ON TAPE
Genesis
Duino Elegies and The Sonnets to Orpheus
The Gospel According to Jesus
The Enlightened Mind
The Enlightened Heart
Letters to a Young Poet
Parables and Portraits
Tao Te Ching
The Book of Job
Selected Poems of Rainer Maria Rilke

GENESIS

A New Translation of the Classic Biblical Stories

by Stephen Mitchell

HarperCollins*Publishers*

FIRST EDITION

Designed and produced by David Bullen

Library of Congress Cataloging-in-Publication Data

Bible. O.T. Genesis. English. Mitchell. 1996.
Genesis/a new translation [and commentary] of the classic biblical stories by Stephen Mitchell.
p. cm.
Includes bibliographical references.
ISBN 0-06-017249-5
1. Bible. O.T. Genesis—Commentaries. 2. Bible stories.—O.T. Genesis.
BS1233.M57 1996
222'.1107—dc20   96-16566
96 97 98 99 00 ❖/RRD 10 9 8 7 6 5 4 3 2 1

To Norman Lear

Contents

On Translating Genesis

I

I had no intention of translating Genesis until, on the day before the Fourth of July, 1994, Bill Moyers called and invited me to participate in his PBS series. I told him I would think about it and get back to him in three days.

Actually, it wasn't thinking that I did during those three days. It was a kind of alert waiting.

> Do you have the patience to wait
>> till your mud settles and the water is clear?
> Can you remain unmoving
>> till the right action arises by itself?

I knew that much of Genesis spoke to me without intimacy, in the tones of a stranger; much of it didn't speak to me at all. If the fellow inside who makes my decisions required a wholehearted love for the book as a prerequisite, I would have to say no.

I soon realized that this was a matter of affinity. If I could find even one passage in Genesis where I had the kind of umbilical connection that I felt with the *Job* poet, or with Rilke or Lao-tzu, that might be enough. During the first hour of musing on the question,

I found five. There was the verse at the end of chapter 1 when God calls the world "very good": a verse that had lit up for me in the mid-seventies, after several years of intensive meditation, as the perfect metaphor for the spaciousness of a mind in which repose and insight are synonymous. Then, Abram's response to the call in chapter 12, a paradigm for every spiritual departure. There was the story of Jacob and Rachel, especially 29:20 ("And Jacob served seven years for Rachel; and they seemed to him just a few days, so great was his love for her"), a verse that described a crucial aspect of my own inner practice and was — is — for me the most moving verse in the entire Bible. "Jacob and the (So-Called) Angel," an enormously important story while I was training with my old Zen master, showed me that not only wrestling with but defeating God is a necessary rite of passage to spiritual freedom. And finally the great "Joseph and His Brothers," a story of descent, transformation, and mastery, with an insight-filled, all-embracing forgiveness at its core. In addition, I had long been fascinated with Adam, Eve, and the serpent, and with "The Binding of Isaac": profound, brilliant stories that rise from the depths of the unconscious mind, uncensored, unfiltered, dark, rich, unassimilable, compelling, and dangerous if taken at surface value — the first one, as interpreted by the Church, a catastrophe in the history of our culture; both of them crying out for midrash, creative transformation, to make them true.

So the deep connections were there, and I knew that I could accept the invitation with a sense of integrity. But the process felt incomplete, as if one more step was necessary. That step appeared at the end of the second day. If I agreed to talk about Genesis, I would first have to translate it: to confront it in its entirety, immerse myself in it, live with it in the kind of intimacy that the process of translation requires. Once I had done that, I would know it through and through, the way Adam knew Eve. Even if there were things about it that I disliked, it would have become part of me, and I could dislike these things from the inside.

I had no illusions about the actual work of translation. Some of it would be interesting. Some of it would be exquisitely dull — the genealogies written by P, the Priestly Writer (that adding machine among poets); the absurd patchwork of "Abram and the Kings," which I would have to translate into an equally clumsy English; the late, shoddy accounts of Joseph in power that are stapled onto what Tolstoy called the most beautiful story in the world. None of the work would have the fascination of what's difficult, the passionate challenge of translating great poetry. But I was sure that I would learn a lot.

The mud had settled, considerately on schedule. I called Bill Moyers and said yes.

II

The great Russian poet Boris Pasternak identified the central issue in the art of translation when he said, "The average translator gets the literal meaning right but misses the tone; and tone is everything." This is just as true of prose as of poetry. Tone is the life-rhythm of a mind. Reading a translation that renders a great writer's words without re-creating their tone is like listening to a computer play Mozart.

My method in establishing the tone of this Genesis was to listen to the Hebrew with one ear and with the other ear to hear into existence an equivalent English. In the process I had to filter out the sound of the King James Version, insofar as that is possible. English-speaking readers usually think of biblical language as Elizabethan: magniloquent, orotund, liturgical, archaic, full of *thees* and *thous* and *untos* and *thereofs* and *prays*. But ancient Hebrew, especially ancient Hebrew prose, is in many ways the opposite of that. Its dignity comes from its supreme simplicity. It is a language of concision and powerful earthiness, austere in its vocabulary, straightforward in its syntax, spare with its adjectives and adverbs — a language that pulses with the energy of elemental human truths.

My job was to re-create this massive dignity and simplicity in an English that felt like it was mine. Dignity is not, I think, a quality you can aim at; it is a function of a writer's sincerity, and it arises on its own in a translation if you have listened deeply enough to the original text and have at the same time been faithful to the genius of the English language. Simplicity is a bit easier to talk about. It doesn't only mean using as few words as possible. It is also a matter of finding a language that sounds completely natural, unliterary, in some sense unwritten: the words of a voice telling ancient stories without adornment and without self-consciousness. This biblical style is a creation of the highest literary intuition and tact. No other Western classic has anything like it. It is worlds away from the exquisitely precise, elaborated, gorgeous language of the Homeric poems, the other great texts at the source of Western culture.

The translation of prose, almost as much as of poetry, requires an ear finely attuned to the sound of words. It is fatal when a contemporary Genesis confuses the natural with the vulgar or imitates the

<INTRODUCTION>

cadences of the King James Version. Stiff formality is one extreme, vulgar breeziness the other; in Dryden's terms, you must be neither on stilts nor too low. But finding the right tone is not a question of testing the levels of diction the way Goldilocks tested the mattresses, of finding the midpoint between high and low. You can't measure tone with a ruler or a compass. You have to find the sound of the genuine.

> It has to be living, to learn the speech of the place.
> It has to face the men of the time and to meet
> The women of the time.

Over the next few months, as I worked on Genesis and began to talk about it, people kept asking, "How is your translation different from other translations?" (I felt I was always responding to the question of the youngest son on the first night of Passover.) I tried to explain by quoting Pasternak on tone. If someone persisted and showed real interest, I would sit him down with three other versions of some central passages and let him compare for himself. This is the most direct way.

In the following excerpts the first entry is from the Revised English Bible, the best of the committee versions; the second is from E. A. Speiser's Anchor Bible *Genesis*; the third is by Everett Fox; the fourth is mine.

The first passage is the beginning of the dialogue between Eve and the serpent. Here everything depends on the genuineness of the spoken word. The serpent must sound colloquial, offhand, devious almost in passing. He is not asking Eve a question; he is, delicately, insidiously, arousing her curiosity; his first speech is nothing but a raised eyebrow. Eve, on the other hand, has to speak with the syntax and the innocence of a child.

> The serpent, which was the most cunning of all the creatures the LORD God had made, asked the woman, "Is it true that God has forbidden you to eat from any tree in the garden?" She replied, "We may eat the fruit of any tree in the garden, except for the tree in the middle of the garden. God has forbidden us to eat the fruit of that tree or even to touch it; if we do, we shall die." "Of course you will not die," said the serpent; "for God knows that, as soon as you eat it, your eyes will be opened, and you will be like God himself, knowing both good and evil." The woman looked at the tree: the fruit would be good to eat; and it was pleasing to the eye and desirable for the knowledge it could give. So she took some and ate it; she also gave some to her husband, and he ate it.
>
> REVISED ENGLISH BIBLE [3:1-6]

Now the serpent was the sliest of all the wild creatures that God Yahweh had made. Said he to the woman, "Even though God told you not to eat of any tree in the garden . . ." The woman interrupted the serpent, "But we may eat of the trees in the garden! It is only about the fruit of the tree in the middle of the garden that God did say, 'Do not eat of it or so much as touch it, lest you die!'" But the serpent said to the woman, "You are not going to die. No, God well knows that the moment you eat of it your eyes will be opened and you will be the same as God in telling good from bad."

When the woman saw that the tree was good for eating and a delight to the eye, and that the tree was attractive as a means to wisdom, she took of its fruit and ate; and she gave some to her husband and he ate.

E. A. SPEISER, *Genesis*

Now the snake was more shrewd than all the living-things of the field that YHWH, God, had made. / It said to the woman: / Even though God said: You are not to eat from any of the trees in the garden . . . ! / The woman said to the snake: / From the fruit of the (other) trees in the garden we may eat, / but from the fruit of the tree that is in the midst of the garden, / God has said: You are not to eat from it and you are not to touch it, / lest you die. / The snake said to the woman: / Die, you will not die! / Rather, God knows / that on the day that you eat from it, your eyes will be opened / and you will become like gods, knowing good and evil. / The woman saw / that the tree was good for eating / and that it was a delight to the eyes, / and the tree was desirable to contemplate. / She took from its fruit and ate / and gave also to her husband beside her, / and he ate.

> EVERETT FOX, *The Five Books of Moses* (the diagonal lines used here do not appear in the Fox version; they indicate where new lines in that version begin, as if the passage were verse)

Now the serpent was more cunning than any creature the Lord had made. And he said to the woman, "Did God really say that you're not allowed to eat from any tree in the garden?"

And the woman said, "We *are* allowed to eat from any tree in the garden. It's just the tree in the middle of the garden that we must not eat from, because God said, 'If you eat from it, or even touch it, you die.'"

And the serpent said, "You will not die. God knows that as soon as you eat from it, your eyes will be opened, and you will be like gods, knowing good and evil."

And when the woman saw that the tree was good to eat from and beautiful to look at, she took one of its fruits and ate, and gave it to her husband, and he ate too.

> STEPHEN MITCHELL

My second example is from "The Destruction of Sodom and Gomorrah." This story is horrifying in several ways, not the least of which is the author's unconsciousness of the casual brutality of Lot's offer; Lot is, after all, considered a righteous man and a paradigm of hospitality, and the prose barely shudders when he volunteers his virgin daughters to be raped by the mob. Here again, for the dialogue to work, the English has to be natural and passionate: Lot must make his offer, in the panic of the moment, with the simplest of words; the mob must *sound* like a mob, shouting real threats, not phrases that would never be heard except in the soundproof chambers of a translator's mind.

> But before they had lain down to sleep, the men of Sodom, both old and young, everyone without exception, surrounded the house. They called to Lot: "Where are the men who came to you tonight? Bring them out to us, so that we may have intercourse with them." Lot went out into the doorway to them, and, closing the door behind him, said, "No, my friends, do not do anything so wicked. Look, I have two daughters, virgins both of them; let me bring them out to you, and you can do what you like with them. But do nothing to these men, because they have come under the shelter of my roof." They said, "Out of our way! This fellow has come and settled here as an alien, and does he now take it upon himself to judge us? We will treat you worse than them." They crowded in on Lot, and pressed close to break down the door. But the two men inside reached out, pulled Lot into the house, and shut the door. Then they struck those in the doorway, both young and old, with blindness so that they could not find the entrance.
>
> R. E. B. [19:4-11]

Before they could lie down, the townspeople, the men of Sodom, young and old — all the people to the last man — closed in on the house. They called out to Lot and said to him, "Where are the men who came to you tonight? Bring them out to us that we may get familiar with them." Lot met them outside at the entrance, having shut the door behind him. He said, "I beg you, my friends, don't be wicked. Look, I have two daughters who never consorted with a man. Let me bring them out to you, and you may do to them as you please. But don't do anything to these men, inasmuch as they have come under the shelter of my roof." They answered, "Stand back! The fellow," they said, "came here on sufferance, and now he would act the master! Now we'll be meaner to you than to them!" With that, they pressed hard against the person of Lot and moved forward to break down the door. But the men put out their hands and pulled Lot inside, shutting the door. And the people who were at the entrance of the house, one and all, they struck with blinding light, so that they were unable to reach the entrance.

SPEISER

They had not yet lain down, when the men of the city, the men of Sedom, encircled the house, / from young lad to old man, all the people (even) from the outskirts. / They called out to Lot and said to him: / Where are the men who came to you tonight? / Bring them out to us, we want to know them! / Lot went out to them, to the entrance, shutting the door behind him / and said: Pray, brothers, do not be so wicked! / Now pray, I have two daughters who have never known a man, / pray let me bring them out to you, and you may deal with them however seems good in your eyes; / only to these men do nothing, / for they have, after all, come under the shadow of my roof-beam! / But they said: / Step aside! / and said: / This one came here to sojourn, and here he would act-the-judge and adjudicate?! / Now we will treat you more wickedly than them! / And they pressed exceedingly hard against the man, against Lot, and stepped closer to break down the door. / But the men put out their hand and brought Lot in to them, into the house, and shut the door. / And the men who were at the entrance to the house, they struck with dazzling-light, (all men) great and small, / so that they were unable to find the entrance.

FOX

Before they had gone to bed, the men of Sodom surrounded the house, young and old, down to the last man. And they called out to Lot, "Where are the men who came to you tonight? Bring them out here, so we can sleep with them."

And Lot went out into the entrance and shut the door behind him. And he said, "Friends, I beg you, don't do this wicked thing. Look, I have two daughters who have never slept with a man. Let me bring them out, and you can do whatever you want to them. But don't do anything to these men, because they have come under the shelter of my roof."

And someone said, "Out of our way!" And someone said, "This fellow just got here, and now he is telling us what to do! Watch out, or you'll get it even worse than them!" And they pressed hard against Lot and moved in closer, to break down the door. But the beings reached out and pulled Lot inside and shut the door. And they struck the men at the entrance with a dazzling light, so that no one could find the door.

MITCHELL

The last passage I will quote for comparison is the climactic scene in the Joseph story, one of the most moving passages in the entire Bible. Joseph's reaction is conveyed in the Hebrew with immense power, yet with the greatest delicacy imaginable. An error in tone here, a weak noun, an unconscious rhyme, falsifies the deep emotion and brings the scene perilously close to melodrama or farce.

> When Joseph looked around, he saw his own mother's son, his brother Benjamin, and asked, "Is this your youngest brother, of whom you told me?" and to Benjamin he said, "May God be gracious to you, my son." Joseph, suddenly overcome by his feelings for his brother, was almost in tears, and he went into the inner room and wept. Then, having bathed his face, he came out and, with his feelings now under control, he ordered the meal to be served.
>
> R. E. B. [43:29-31]

> As his eye fell on Benjamin, his mother's son, he asked, "Is this the youngest brother of whom you spoke to me?" And he added, "God be gracious to you, my boy." With that, Joseph hurried out, for he was overcome with feeling for his brother, and wanted to cry. He went into a room and wept there. Then he washed his face and reappeared and — now in control of himself again — gave the order, "Serve the meal!"
>
> SPEISER

> He lifted up his eyes and saw Binyamin his brother, his mother's son, / and he said: / Is this your youngest brother, of whom you spoke to me? / And he said: / May God show you favor, my son! / And in haste — for his feelings were so kindled toward his brother that he had to weep —/ Yosef entered a chamber and wept there. / Then he washed his face and came out, he restrained himself, and said: / Serve bread!
>
> FOX

And Joseph looked at his brother Benjamin, his own mother's son, and said, "This must be your youngest brother, whom you said you would bring to me." And he said, "May God be gracious to you, my son." And he hurried out: his heart was overwhelmed with love for his brother, and he could no longer hold back his tears. And he went to his room and wept.

Then he washed his face, and composed himself, and came out and said, "Serve the meal."

MITCHELL

III

Gradually, as I settled into the scholarly research essential for translating a biblical text, I realized that there was an item on my agenda that I had barely been conscious of when I began the project. This item became clear for me one day when my friend Diana said, "You're writing a new translation of Genesis? Well, do everyone a favor and for God's sake change that awful story about Eve being to blame for all our misery." "I wish I could," I said. And suddenly I felt how much I really did wish I could.

But translating a biblical text is a very different venture from creating an adaptation of it, as I had done in *A Book of Psalms*. An adaptation of the Genesis stories, while it might be a worthy venture, was not this venture. My job was to *translate* Genesis, using all the considerable help that Hebrew philology and contemporary textual scholarship could provide. But in the back of my mind, as I realized when Diana made her request, I was hoping for discoveries. Especially about Eve. Perhaps in the standard Hebrew text there was a passage that scholars had identified as a much later addition,

and once it was removed, the whole story would be radically transformed. Or a Hebrew word that had been misunderstood for two
thousand years, and once the correct understanding was reached,
Eve, the mother of us all, would be revealed, naked, innocent, chew-
ing with delight on the fruit of the tree in the middle of the garden,
her eyes opened to a live and sinuous wisdom, with no *culpa* (*felix* or
otherwise) projected onto her.

That kind of discovery had happened a number of times as I
worked on the Book of Job — most dramatically in Job's last words,
which are the last words of the great poem that forms the central
panel of the book. The King James, followed by all the other versions, translates verse 42:6 as "Wherefore I abhor myself, and
repent in dust and ashes." I had a powerful intuitive sense that this
could not be right, that Job's vision was worth nothing if it had not
illuminated his heart, and that a supremely great poet like the
author of *Job* would never have had his hero end up in a puddle of
self-abasement. And this intuition was confirmed when I discovered that three Hebrew words had been consistently misunderstood, and that the verse actually meant "Therefore I will be quiet, /
comforted that I am dust." Thus, as I had felt sure, Job's final speech
issues not from mere capitulation to superior force but from wholehearted spiritual surrender, and is an appropriate conclusion to the
Voice from the Whirlwind's fierce, compassionate, dazzling non-
answer.

I made no discoveries of this importance in the Eve story, alas.
But I did find, throughout Genesis, a considerable number of words
that had been elucidated in the pages of scholarly books and jour-
nals, words that most translators had not understood with enough

precision. These clarifications change the texture of some of the most important stories.

Three examples. In chapter 16, Hagar runs away into the wilderness.

> And Sarai treated her harshly, and she ran away. And the Lord found her near a spring in the wilderness, the spring on the way to Shur. [16:6-7]

In all translations it is "the angel of the Lord" who finds Hagar; and, in fact, the word *mal'akh* always does mean "angel" in later Hebrew. But in early Hebrew, when the word was more fluid, it means something like "manifestation," which can take the form either of a being who is separate from the Lord or of the Lord himself. We know that the character here is not an angel because of verse 13, in which Hagar acknowledges that she spoke with and saw the Lord himself. And there are a number of other texts in Genesis and Exodus where the word has the same meaning; sometimes the *mal'akh* even says "I am the God of Beth-El" or "I will make him into a great nation." So the precisely accurate translation here is "And the Presence of the Lord found her" or "And the Lord-as-manifested (on earth) found her" or, more simply, "And the Lord found her." The whole story seems more intimate, more poignant, when it is the Lord himself rather than his messenger who comes down into the wilderness to help the abused slave-girl. This is true also in "The Binding of Isaac," where, in spite of Rembrandt, in spite of a thousand Renaissance paintings, it is God himself who at the last moment calls to Abraham to prevent him from slaughtering his son.

This clarification is related to another philological nicety in "Abraham and the Three Visitors" and "Jacob and the 'Angel.'" The

Hebrew word *'ish* usually means "man." But in the context of chapters 18 and 19 it means "(superhuman) being," and it is important to translate it that way.

> And the Lord appeared to Abraham by the great oaks of Mamre as he sat before his tent in the heat of the day. And he looked up and saw three beings standing near him. [18:1-2]

Though their appetites are capable of doing justice to Abraham's huge feast—an entire roast calf, yogurt, milk, and several hundred pita breads—these three beings are not human; one of them is actually the Lord himself. In the same way, it is God whom Jacob defeats in the famous wrestling match.

> And Jacob was left alone; and a being [*'ish*] wrestled with him until dawn. [32:25]

We learn that the being is neither a human nor an angel when he tells Jacob, "Your name will . . . be . . . Israel [*He Who Has Struggled with God*] because you have struggled with God and you have won." (In this verse, after "struggled with God," a scandalized editor added the phrase "and with men" to weaken the assertion of a victory over God.) Realizing who his opponent is, Jacob names the place Penuel [*The Face of God*]: "because I have seen God face to face, yet my life has been spared."

A more subtle clarification occurs at the end of "The Betrothal of Rebecca," when, arriving in the Negev after her journey from Mesopotamia, Rebecca sees Isaac for the first time.

> And Rebecca looked up, and when she saw Isaac, she leaned down from her camel and asked the slave, "Who is that man walking toward us?" [24:64-65]

In understanding this verse I have used the erratic but sometimes brilliant philological intuition of the early-twentieth-century German-Jewish scholar Arnold B. Ehrlich, whose *Randglossen zur Hebräischen Bibel* is both a treasure trove and a junk heap. Ehrlich wrote:

> The verb *va-tipol* does not mean "she dismounted," as people usually translate it, following the Septuagint (the primary ancient Greek version of the Bible — s. m.). This translation is mistaken, because no woman can dismount from a camel (unassisted, because of its height and her clothing — s. m.), especially when the animal is moving, as it is here. Onkelos (another ancient translator, into Aramaic — s. m.) gave the correct translation: "she leaned down." . . . Isaac had already come fairly near, and so that he might not hear what she said, Rebecca leaned from her high seat on the camel down to the slave who was walking beside it, in order to whisper the question to him.

It is a lovely refinement in the story if — rather than see Rebecca jump or slide down from the camel, an action that, even granted its possibility, would surely have been considered crude and improper — we see her leaning down over the camel's neck to whisper her passionately interested question to the slave.

The third example is a crucial verse in "Cain and Abel."

> And the Lord accepted Abel and his offering; but Cain and his offering he didn't accept. And Cain was very troubled, and his face fell. [4:5]

Most translations say that Cain was "very angry." But the Hebrew phrase here, *ḥarah l-*, indicates mental anguish, not anger, which is expressed by the similar phrase *ḥarah 'af*. Cain is not angry: his face has fallen, he is troubled and depressed, as well he might be. This makes him a slightly more sympathetic character.

There are many such philological subtleties in Genesis, and they are important to recognize in the spare vocabulary of ancient Hebrew, where the same word can have dozens of different nuances. A clearer understanding of even one word can change the whole texture of a story.

IV

When people asked how this translation is different from the others, there was one other matter that I would sometimes explain to them. This explanation involves a lesson in textual scholarship. I will make it brief.

The stories in Genesis were composed, some of them from ancient folk material, by a number of different writers, as biblical scholars have established beyond a doubt. There are at least four writers, and probably half a dozen more: J, the author of many of the most famous stories in Genesis (J for Yahwist, or Jahwist in its German spelling, so called because he almost always uses the name *YHVH*, "the Lord," for God); E, whose greatest story is "The Binding of Isaac" (E for Elohist, because he uses the name *Elohim*, "God" in a curious, seemingly plural form, for God); P, the Priestly Writer; the author of "Joseph and His Brothers"; and a number of other writers whom I call "early sources" and "late sources." In addition, there was an editor, known as R (for Redactor), who collected all these texts and tried to reconcile them and make one continuous narrative out of the disparate sources. The (very approximate) dates of these writers are: J, 950-800 B.C.E.; E, 850-750; P, 700-500; the Joseph author, 1000-900; early sources, 950-750; late sources, after 587; and R, 450-400.

If there is any author of Genesis as a whole, it is R. He was in certain ways a very skillful editor, and I will discuss the shape of his book in the last section of this essay. But Genesis as it is presented to us in R's recension — as we read it in the Hebrew text and in all the translations, except for a few scholarly ones — is a disservice to the original authors. That is why in this book I have separated the text into its sources, printing each story as a distinct work by a particular writer. (For many of these attributions, there is general scholarly consensus. Much of the time I have agreed with the contemporary German scholar Claus Westermann, whose three-volume commentary on Genesis is one of the great works of Hebrew textual scholarship.)

A peculiarity of the text that the present format makes much more obvious is what scholars call doublets: two (sometimes three) versions of the same story, by different authors. There are many doublets in Genesis: "The Creation" according to P and according to J; "The Flood" according to J and according to P; "Wife and Sister" (three versions: J, E, and a late source); "The Promise to Abram" (J and one or possibly two late sources) and "The Covenant with Abraham" (P); "Hagar and Ishmael" according to J and according to E; "Beer-sheba" (three versions: E, J, and a late source); "Why Jacob Was Sent to Laban" according to J ("Esau Cheated of the Blessing") and according to P; "Jacob at Beth-El" according to J and according to E; and "Jacob Becomes Israel" according to J ("Jacob Wrestles with God") and according to P.

In one instance, "The Flood," R took the two versions and combined them into a single text (see Appendix 2). This accounts for
the various discrepancies in the composite story as it is usually translated. In J's story, *the Lord* commands Noah to bring *seven* pairs of all
the ritually clean animals and one pair of all the unclean animals into
the ark, so that afterward Noah can perform an animal sacrifice
without causing the extinction of a species; in P's story, *God* commands Noah to bring just *one* pair of each into the ark. In J's story, it
is *rain* that causes the flood; in P's, the floodwaters issue from both
the upper reservoir ("the floodgates of heaven") *and the subterranean
source* ("the wells of the great deep"). In J's story, the flood lasts for
forty days; in P's, for *a hundred and fifty*. When the two strands are
unwoven, each version becomes clear and self-consistent. We can
also see more easily the distinctive elements in each: in J's story, the
regretful Lord, sorry that he ever created humans, like a righteous
but not wise man who feels heartsick at the corruption and suffering on the front page of his morning newspaper and can barely
repress a wish to blow up the whole world and be done with it, the
ridiculous yet touching detail of having the Lord shut the door of
the ark behind Noah after he has entered with all the animals, the
three flights of the dove (the raven is a variant that I have relegated
to the Textual Notes), and the lovely last sentence — "For as long as
the earth endures, these will not end: seedtime and harvest, cold
and heat, summer and winter, day and night." While in P's story we
find the detailed instructions for building the ark, the various stages
of the rising and subsiding of the waters, the landing on Ararat, and
the promise of the rainbow.

Sometimes one story in the doublet is a very inferior version.

<INTRODUCTION>

This is true, for example, of two of the P stories, "Why Jacob Was Sent to Laban" and "Jacob Becomes Israel." The J versions are among the greatest stories in the Bible, in all literature; but they made an orthodox mind like P's extremely uncomfortable. Just as the early rabbis of the Midrash (and all the later rabbinic commentators, for that matter) change Esau into a villain and rationalize away Jacob's dishonesty and disrespect, P eliminates all the brilliant, troubling, morally ambiguous elements of J's story. "No, no," he seems to be saying, "it wasn't like that at all. Jacob wasn't sent to Mesopotamia because, God forbid, he deceived his father and cheated his brother and was in danger of being killed. It all happened because Esau married two Canaanite women, against the wishes of his parents. So Esau was the bad son. Jacob was the obedient one; he went to Mesopotamia out of filial piety, because his father commanded him to. And he didn't steal the blessing, God forbid; Isaac gave it to him knowingly." In the same way, P's version of "Jacob Becomes Israel," a clumsy story in an indifferent style, eliminates all mention of the wrestling match and simply states the new name without even trying to explain its meaning.

Some of the doublet stories, though very different from each other, are written with almost equal skill. This is most obviously true of the two creation stories. It is also true of the lesser-known "Hagar and Ishmael." E's revision of this story is even more moving than J's original. Like the P version of "Why Jacob Was Sent to Laban," it was written by an author who knew the earlier story and wanted to correct it. What seems to have bothered E most are the portrayals of Sarah and Abraham. J's Sarah is manipulative, insecure, selfish, and harsh to the point of cruelty, while Abraham is a wimp who capitulates to his wife's jealousy and washes his hands of the whole business. Hagar herself, while an object of pity and admiration in her escape to the wilderness, is also seen as the partial cause of her own misfortune. The only character who comes off well is the kindly Lord.

In E's version, Sarah's jealousy and anger are more arbitrary, though just as unpleasant; this immediately establishes Hagar as a more sympathetic figure. But it is especially Abraham whom E is concerned about. He can't change the basic facts, as they were given to him by an already ancient tradition: that Sarah caused Hagar's flight or banishment into the wilderness, that Abraham did nothing to intervene, and that God rescued and comforted Hagar. But E wants to make Abraham less passive and callous, and more of a father to Ishmael. He does this brilliantly, in one sentence: "And this troubled Abraham very greatly, because Ishmael too was his son." The subsequent visit or vision from God achieves two purposes: it legitimizes both Sarah's demand and Abraham's acquiescence, and it takes the danger and therefore Abraham's moral responsibility out of the banishment, since he knows from the start that God "will make (Ishmael) too into a great nation." The next part of E's story, the description of Hagar's departure and of her rescue in the wilderness, is a triumph of tenderness and skill. (Ishmael is obviously a young child here, small enough to be carried on his mother's shoulder, although the story has been spliced into the Genesis narrative four chapters after P's "The Covenant with Abraham," in which Ishmael is already thirteen years old.) And it ends with a version of Ishmael that is strikingly different from J's. Rather than portraying Ishmael as a wild and warlike savage, E makes the remarkable statement that "God was with the boy as he grew up," a statement about a kind of blessedness and charmed existence that is almost unique in Genesis: only of Ishmael and Joseph is this said.

In another doublet, the strange "Wife and Sister" (actually a triplet), E is clumsier in his revisions, probably because the material is more refractory. It is easy to see what disturbed him in J's portrayal of Abram. We can understand the instinct for self-preservation that makes Abram ask Sarai to lie, but self-preserving here is indistinguishable from self-serving. And when J says that Pharaoh took Sarai as a wife, he strongly implies sexual consummation. Abram is well rewarded for his complaisance and seems, to the great discomfort of some contemporary readers, very much like a pimp. In E's revision, the king (not Pharaoh now, but Abimelech of Gerar) takes Sarah into his harem but doesn't have sex with her, as E emphatically states. Not only does he not have sex with her: he *can't* have sex with her, since God has made him impotent. Thus E assures his readers that no impropriety resulted from Abraham's lie. Not only that: according to E the lie wasn't really a lie, since Sarah is Abraham's half-sister. This relationship is unattested in the older tradition; E invents it here, purely for the purpose of defending Abraham's truthfulness. Furthermore, according to E, the king gives Abraham his reward *after* he learns that Sarah is Abraham's wife; it is a compensation and a proof, rather than a finder's fee. (The author of the third and still tamer version is bothered even by hearing that E's Abimelech takes Sarah into his harem; *his* Abimelech gets no closer to Rebecca than seeing her from an upper window.)

As I separated the stories into their sources, I came to feel that there was another, greater disservice that had been done to them and to their authors. By the time they arrived on R's desk, some of the stories—J's, E's, and the Joseph author's—were four or five hundred years old, and much material had been added to them by various scribes in the course of half a millennium. (Westermann's nose for these additions is particularly acute, but there is general scholarly consensus about the more important ones.) The most extraordinary example is "The Rape of Dinah": though the original version ended in the relatively tame murder of the rapist and his men by Simeon and Levi, the later version, taking its cue from the genocidal hatred of Deuteronomy 7, has Jacob's sons murder all the males in the Canaanite city and enslave the women and children (see Appendix 3). But there were many other additions, small and large. R could have had no way of knowing about them or about any original versions. What he had to work with were the texts he was given, which he would have considered sacrosanct.

His sense of the sacred did not, however, prevent him from doing the job of a good editor. He wove together the J and P strands of the Flood story, as we have seen, and in many other instances tried to reconcile the different versions by proper placement and with editorial insertions. To J's version of "Hagar and Ishmael," for example, R added two very clumsy verses.

> And the Lord found her near a spring in the wilderness, the spring on the way to Shur. And he said, "Hagar, where have you come from and where are you going?" And she said, "I am running away from Sarai, my mistress." *And* mal'akh YHVH (which to R would have meant "the angel of the Lord") *said to her, "Go back to your mistress, and submit to her harsh treatment." And* mal'akh YHVH *said to*

her, "I will multiply your descendants very greatly, and they will be too many
to be counted." [16:9-10] And the Lord said to her, "You are pregnant,
and you will give birth to a son, and you will name him Ishmael...."

R's reason for adding the first of these two verses is clear: J's story
left Hagar in the wilderness; R had to get her back to Sarai so that
she could be banished in chapter 21, in E's version, which R would
have considered a later incident in a continuous story.

Often R would splice one or several verses from P into a J story
to establish the chronology, as in J's "The Promise to Abram."

And Abram went, as the Lord had told him to; and Lot went with
him. *And Abram was seventy-five years old when he left Haran. And
Abram took Sarai his wife, and Lot his brother's son, and all their possessions that they had obtained, and the people that they had acquired in
Haran, and they set out for the land of Canaan [12:4b–5]*, and they
arrived in Canaan and passed through the land as far as the sanctuary at Shechem, the great oak of Moreh.

The insertion here is skillful enough, but elsewhere R's splices can
be awkward, interrupting the flow of the narrative and interpolat-
ing P's dull prose into the brilliant concision of J, as at the beginning
of J's "Hagar and Ishmael."

Now Sarai had not borne Abram any children. And she had an
Egyptian maid whose name was Hagar. And Sarai said to Abram,
"See how the Lord has prevented me from bearing children. I beg
you now, go and sleep with my maid, and perhaps I will have a son
through her." And Abram did what Sarai had asked: *And Abram's
wife Sarai took Hagar the Egyptian, her maid, after Abram had lived ten*

years in the land of Canaan, and gave her to Abram her husband as his con-
cubine. [16:3] He slept with Hagar, and she conceived. And when she
knew that she was pregnant ...

Early on in the work of translation, I decided to omit all these
additional verses, whether they had been added by R or by some
scribe centuries before. I felt obliged to do this out of loyalty to J, E,
and the Joseph author, who are the great writers of Genesis. What
author would want his work presented to the public cluttered with
the second and third thoughts of second- and third-rate writers? As
I relegated these accretions to the Textual Notes, the stories took
on a stunning clarity. It was like removing coat after coat of lacquer
that had obscured the vibrant colors of a masterpiece. This was
most impressive in the Joseph story. But there are many other striking examples.

In the original version of "The Binding of Isaac," for example,
God calls to Abraham just once, after which Abraham sees the ram,
sacrifices it, names the place, and leaves. Some scribe, copying passages from elsewhere in Genesis, appended a second heavenly inter-
vention (scholars are virtually unanimous that this is a later addition).

And the angel of the Lord called to Abraham a second time from the sky and
said, "'I swear,' says the Lord, 'that because you have done this, and have not
withheld your son, your darling, I will greatly bless you, and I will greatly
multiply your descendants so that they are as many as the stars in the sky and
the sands on the seashore. And your descendants will seize the gates of their
enemies, and in your descendants all the nations of the earth will be blessed,
because you have obeyed my command.'" [22:15-18]

This awkward and anticlimactic passage is a blot on a story of the greatest economy and tact.

Another clumsy addition occurs at the end of J's "The Destruction of Sodom and Gomorrah." It is a silly passage, written in a style obviously different from the rest of the story, and it interrupts the high drama of the climactic moment.

> And as soon as dawn came, the beings said to Lot, "Hurry, take your wife and the two daughters who are here, or you will be crushed in the punishment of the city." And he still lingered. And the beings took him by the hand, and his wife and the two daughters also, since the Lord was merciful to him, and they led them out and left them outside the city. And one of them said, "Run for your lives! Don't look back, don't stop anywhere in the plain: run to the hills or you will be crushed!"
>
> *And Lot said, "Please don't, sir. You have been so good to me and have shown me such great kindness in saving my life, but if I try to run to the hills, the destruction will overtake me and I will die. Look, that town over there, I can go to it, and it is so small. Please let me go there: it is so small, and my life will be saved." And he said to him, "I will grant you this favor too, and I will not obliterate the town. Hurry, go; for I can't do anything until you get there." That is why the town was named Zoar [Small]. The sun was rising as Lot entered Zoar.* [19:18-23]
>
> And the Lord rained sulfurous fire on Sodom and Gomorrah, and he obliterated those cities, and the whole plain, and all the cities' inhabitants, and everything that grew on the ground.
>
> And Lot's wife looked back, and she turned into a pillar of salt.
>
> And in the morning Abraham went back to the place where he had stood in the Lord's presence. And he looked down toward Sodom and Gomorrah, across the whole plain, and the smoke from it was rising like the smoke from a furnace.

Ehrlich points out that not only is this passage awkward, it makes nonsense of "Lot's Daughters," also by J, which follows it.

> The statement in 19:31, "there are no men left on earth to lie with us," clearly shows that everything that is said about Zoar proceeds from a later hand. Only according to the original story, in which Lot fled directly from Sodom into the hills, can the daughters believe that the whole world had perished as in the Flood; they could not believe this, however, if they had in the meantime been living in Zoar and seen its inhabitants quite alive.

In "Jacob and Esau," two verses have been inserted near the beginning, for a particular purpose.

> Now Rebecca was barren, and Isaac prayed to the Lord for her. And the Lord answered his prayer, and Rebecca conceived. *And the children fought inside her womb; and she said, "If it is like this, why do I live?" And she went to consult the Lord's oracle. And the Lord said to her:*
>> *"Two nations are in your womb,*
>>> *two peoples inside your body.*
>> *But one shall be stronger than the other*
>>> *and the elder shall serve the younger."* [25:22-23]
>
> And when it was time for her to give birth, twins came out of her womb. And the first one was red and hairy like a fur cloak; so they named him Esau [*The Shaggy One*]. And then his brother came out, with one hand grasping Esau's heel; so they named him Jacob [*Heel-Grasper*].

The continuation of this story, "Esau Cheated of the Blessing," causes problems for any reader who wants to see Jacob as a decent, honest man. Whether or not Rebecca and he are right in thinking that the end justifies the means, their deceit is deeply unsavory. The author of these two inserted verses must have felt so troubled by the story that he had to authorize Rebecca's preference for Jacob by enlisting God on her side. But in its original version, with the oracle removed, it is a simpler, more powerful story of how Rebecca loved Jacob and Isaac loved Esau. God plays no part in it at all.

Of all the texts, "Joseph and His Brothers" is the one that most dramatically benefits when we leave out the accretions. Unlike the rest of Genesis, the Joseph story seems to be a unified whole, by a single author of genius. As Westermann has written, "The Joseph narrative as far as chapter 45 runs its course in a continuous, coherent, and clearly arranged sequence of events; the conclusion, chapters 46-50, is complicated. It contains expansions, doublings, breaks in continuity, and much that does not seem to belong immediately to the Joseph narrative." I have relegated these additions to Appendix 1. They are all dull or awkward (except for "The Testament of Jacob," which is a skillful early poem, though not nearly as good as the best biblical poetry), and they seriously interfere with the flow of the narrative. The worst of them are "Joseph's Land Policy," in which Joseph's enslavement of the Egyptians is an unconsciously, chillingly ironic precursor of Exodus 1, and the ludicrous "Joseph and His Brothers Reconciled."

> And when Joseph's brothers realized that their father was dead, they said, "What if Joseph still bears a grudge against us and takes revenge on us for all the harm we did to him?" So they sent this message to Joseph: "Your father gave us this message before he died: 'Say this to Joseph: "Forgive, I beg you, the crime and sin of your brothers, who did you harm."' So now, please, forgive the crime of the servants of the God of your father." And Joseph wept at their words to him. [50:15-17]

It is indeed hard to keep from weeping at these words, so clumsy and bathetic are they. How any writer could have had the gall to add them to the impeccable prose of the Joseph story is beyond comprehension.

V

The God of Genesis is a human creation, not the God at the center of the universe. Whenever God is presented as a character, that presentation is partial, therefore false. God is not a character in a story. God is the whole story.

Words such as *God* and *Tao* and *Buddha-nature* only point to the reality that is the source and essence of all things, the luminous intelligence that shines from the depths of the human heart. The ancient Jews named this unnamable reality YHVH, "that which causes (everything) to exist," or, even more insightfully, *ehyéh*, "I am." Yet God is neither here nor there, neither before nor after, neither outside nor inside. As soon as we say that God is God, or even that God is, we have missed it. Lao-tzu said, in his wonderfully forthright way:

> There was something formless and perfect
> before the universe was born.
> It is serene. Empty.
> Solitary. Unchanging.
> Infinite. Eternally present.
> It is the mother of the universe.
> For lack of a better name,
> I call it the Tao.

All words about God are inadequate, but some words are more adequate than others. The Genesis stories have much to teach us about the soul but little to teach us about what the soul longs for. Like all soul stories, they use the character called "God" or "the Lord" to suggest another dimension to this human life of ours. God here is a kind of depth perspective.

There are three presentations of God as a character in Genesis that seem less inadequate than the others. The first is, amazingly, the God of chapter 1. Amazingly, because P is usually a dullard, excessively concerned with external form, genealogy, and ritual. But P's *Elohim* is not yet quite differentiated into the patriarchal God who appears in the other Genesis stories. The human analogy for this God is the artist. The impetus to create comes in the first verse, suddenly, without reason, out of the blue, from an unstoppable urge to make something beautiful or good (the Hebrew word for "good" includes what we would call "beautiful" as well). And at the end of the story, we have the sense of the whole as being more than the sum of its parts. After calling most of the parts "good," God ends the sixth day and enters the Sabbath mind by calling the whole world "*very* good." But the Hebrew word that we translate as "Sabbath" and "rest" implies more than ordinary repose. It implies the overbrimming fullness and joy that a woman feels after she has given birth, the deep fulfillment that an artist has after creating a work of art that perfectly expresses his sense of the world: when he looks at what he has imagined and is astonished at how utterly it is him and yet other than him, something he always knew and yet could never have known before he created it. (When, several years ago, I adapted the creation story for children, rather than being literal with 2:3 as I

was in this translation, I tried to suggest this deeper sense of fulfillment by saying, "And God blessed the seventh day and made it holy.
And in God's joy was all the work of creation.")

The other presentations of God that reflect spiritual truths are
also images of Abraham, since God appears to him as two almost
impossibly painful demands: the voice tells him to leave his family,
his land, everything he knows, and later tells him to sacrifice his
beloved child. "The Binding of Isaac" is an especially rich and difficult story. On its surface, as a story about someone who is commanded by an external God to kill his son as a test of loyalty, it is,
for all its great beauty, a lie. God does not command murder. Nor is
unquestioning obedience necessarily a spiritual virtue. On this level
the story is an authoritarian fable that could have been written by
Eliphaz, Bildad, or Zophar. But at a deeper, metaphorical level it is
a blood-chilling depiction of what surrender can be like: the central
story of any spiritual practice. Anyone can say, "Let go of everything, even of what you love best"; it is a rare achievement for a
writer to shape that truth into the flesh and blood of human char-
acters and to bring us into the center of the experience, the dead
center, absolute zero.

A story that is like it, though much gentler, is the episode in the
life of Guatama when the Buddha-to-be is about to slip out of the
palace. He knows with great certainty that he has to leave his wife
and son behind, knows that if he can wake up to the ultimate truth,
all beings on earth, all beings in infinite dimensions, will benefit
from his awakening, and that if he doesn't leave this won't be possible. So his heartbreaking, compassionate choice is to abandon the
two people whom he loves with all his heart. He stops at the thresh-

old of his wife's bedroom and looks at her sleeping form. He can barely keep himself from stepping into the room and kissing her cheek one last time, one last time taking the child into his arms. But if he stays for even one more moment, he knows he will never leave.

That story has a sweet poignance to it; it is acceptable in a sense in which the Abraham story goes deeply against the grain. We can without too much difficulty imagine what the Buddha had to endure. But we can't imagine the Abraham story unless we have lived it. It comes from a deeper level of the soul; it is richer than the Buddha story because it is darker. It is not simply a story about letting go of attachments. It is about being able, in our depths, to kill what we love best, to snuff out our dearest hope for the future of the world because our dearest hope is still an illusion, to surrender to sheer horror if life swerves into the horrible, to love God with all our heart even when God seems as cruel as the devil. The point at which what we are given is difficult beyond enduring is a point that pierces and refines the soul. And (though this may be hard to believe) it is possible to be so fluid and centered, so filled with trust in the intelligence of the universe, that even horror can pass through us and eventually be transformed into light.

VI

As I hope you will see, the stories in Genesis gain immeasurably in clarity and power when they are separated into their sources rather than read as the artificially continuous narrative created by the Redactor. E's Abraham is not J's Abraham; but while it is inappropriate to think of E's as the same character grown more compassionate in the course of a few years, the two have family resemblances as important as their differences. And simply by being placed beside one another in the same book, all the stories become part of a larger story. It is important to understand what that story is.

Genesis as we know it, that patchwork of disparate styles, has an overall shape that reflects R's keen editorial intelligence. His splices may often be awkward; his inclusion of some material may be ill-judged; but his esthetic intuition is in certain ways admirable. When we consider Genesis in its entirety, we can see that it takes the form of the central story of the human spirit, progressing from original harmony through brokenness and suffering to a deeply moving reconciliation at the end.

It is arbitrary, of course, to consider Genesis as a separate book. Genesis is meant to be a part of a larger whole: of the Torah, or of the entire Hebrew Bible, or of the Christian Bible, or of the Muslim holy books, or of the canon of Jewish sacred texts. As the first book of the Hebrew or the Christian Bible, it concludes with either Second Chronicles or Revelation, both of them unworthy conclusions. A much more appropriate conclusion to Genesis would be either the Book of Job, with its magnificent final vision, or, even better, the Song of Songs — a reentry past the kerubs (those human-headed bulls with eagles' wings), past the fiery whirling sword, into the garden of innocence and sexual joy; a book with not a single mention of God, because God is the garden, God is the joy.

Genesis was never meant to exist by itself, as a self-contained text. However triumphantly and harmoniously it ends, trouble waits just beyond the horizon. Joseph forgives his brothers, the

<INTRODUCTION>

famine is contained, Jacob dies in peace, and everything turns out happily. But not happily ever after. If we take even one step past the last verse of chapter 50, we find ourselves immersed in the slavery and suffering of darkest Egypt. The solution of one problem has sown the seeds of the next.

Nevertheless, if we look at Genesis as a book complete in itself, we will find that it has a shape of remarkable significance and beauty. This was the element that excited and moved me most deeply as I was finishing the translation: the harmony with which Genesis ends, its sense of its own torn beginnings, the metaphorical awareness with which it comes to closure.

R wisely chose the P account of creation as chapter 1. (It is hard to see how he could have reversed the order of the two stories and moved from J's kindly, jealous, bungling god to the relative majesty of P's creator — though the move from P to J is itself bumpy.) There is no sense here of Before the Beginning, of "something formless and perfect / before the universe was born." The curtain rises at *In* the Beginning. God is already a character, the world has been divided into creator and created, and the divisions proceed from one day to the next. The mood is one of great, methodical exuberance. Everything is in order, everything issues from the immense creative power of God, as if we were living in a world where there is only one *I Ching* hexagram: the first. When we enter the Sabbath mind at the end of the sixth day, all is serenity and joy.

Eden is a different story, of course. It begins with the Lord's curiosity and tenderness, continues with the hilarious episode of his trying to find a mate for Adam ("How about this giraffe? No?

Hmm . . . Okay, how about this ocelot?"), and ends in transgression and banishment. The ending is not a cosmic disaster, though; J and the other writers of Genesis, who were comfortable with death and found Abraham's trust in God perfectly sufficient, would have been appalled, as Jesus himself would have been, at the narrowhearted Augustinian interpretation of this story, which Christianity is only now recovering from — that Adam's transgression was an original, all-inclusive sin and that from then on all human beings were corrupt and damned to hell unless they believed in Christ.

Eve is the character in the story who makes the rest of Genesis possible, who acts out of a love for God, if God is wisdom. It is significant that the Lord puts the tree right in the middle of the garden, that he creates the serpent, that he creates Eve with her curiosity. It is a setup for something to happen, as in those fairy tales in which the hero is warned about The One Forbidden Room. God doesn't hide the jar of magic cookies in the attic, he puts it right on the kitchen table. Consciously he hopes his children will obey, but unconsciously he is making it very unlikely. The intelligence of the story wants something to go wrong. In this sense, the serpent is cousin to *Job*'s Accuser, who is, after all, one of the loyal functionaries in God's court. Each in his own way is a truth-teller; each is the dynamic presence who gets the story moving, the dark, unconscious mind of a very unconscious god. You can see them as evil, but that is just a moralized view. As Blake said, "Energy is eternal delight." And it is appropriate that it should be a serpent who embodies this distrust of prohibitions and authority: in many cultures the snake is a wisdom figure and a symbol of immortality, since it sheds its skin and thus is born again. It is a figure for the sinuous, ferociously intelligent vital energy—kundalini—that can flow through a human body and be experienced as a great opening into God.

J's Eden story is meant to explain a fundamental human question: how did it come about that we lost the radiance of childhood, the clouds of glory; how is it that, after living so close to God when we were born, we somehow find ourselves in a consciousness of separation and loss? In truth, if there is any fall, it is a fall into adult consciousness, and that is as much a rise as a fall. We may feel nostalgic for childhood, but the departure from Eden is a necessary one. If we try to be too safe, we can't find our wisdom; we have to be initiated into the world, to enter it and be damaged; people who haven't fully risked that damage can't even begin to develop as spiritual beings. We have to go through the intense pain of separation and somehow integrate that, and then we have to walk into the fiery sword and be burnt or hacked to pieces before we can reenter the garden, not only with a regained innocence but with our adult awareness as well. (That is what Jesus meant when he said, "You must become *like* children to enter the kingdom of God." He didn't say you must become children.)

After Eden, Genesis presents us with a world of great discord and suffering. Almost immediately, jealousy gives rise to fratricide, the first murder. This sets the theme for the rest of the book. The human drama of Genesis centers upon the favoritism of parents and the resulting enmity of brothers.

J's "Cain and Abel" originated as a folktale in a culture of nomadic shepherds, who felt superior to farming cultures and projected that feeling onto their tribal deity as a preference on his part. Even after the story's cultural roots have disappeared, this intensely partisan god remains.

> After a while Cain brought the first fruits of his harvest as an offering to the Lord, and Abel brought the fattest pieces of the firstlings from his flock. And the Lord accepted Abel and his offering; but Cain and his offering he didn't accept. And Cain was very troubled, and his face fell. [4:3-5]

Of *course* Cain was troubled. There was nothing wrong with his offering. Daddy didn't love him.

There are two particularly striking elements here. One is the Lord's partiality, which, uncaused by the goodness or badness of the brothers or of their offerings, is the direct cause of Cain's distress and the indirect cause of the murder. This is the first instance in Genesis of the parental favoritism that is responsible for so much suffering and conflict throughout the book. The Lord favors Abel over Cain, Sarah favors Isaac over Ishmael, Isaac loves Esau while Rebecca loves Jacob, Jacob himself loves Joseph above his other sons. All of them, the Lord included, are blind to the first rule of parenthood: that however much you may personally prefer one of your children to the others, you must love them all equally. This favoritism makes its destructive way from one generation of patriarchs to the next, breeding jealousy and near-violence in every generation.

The second element is J's portrayal of Cain. He is not an unsympathetic character. On the contrary, his hurt and, after the murder, his grief are given eloquent voice.

And Cain said, "My punishment is greater than I can bear. You have banished me from this land, and I must submit to you and become a restless wanderer on the earth, and anyone who meets me can kill me." [4:13-14]

J presents Cain's anguish and restlessness of spirit not as an object of moral condemnation but with a clear-sighted perception of the inner consequences of his crime. ("Men are not punished *for* their sins, but *by* them.") In the same way, later in the book, we feel the pain of Esau when he cries out loudly and bitterly and says, "Bless me, bless me too, Father." That cry echoes down through the families of all generations.

The largest consciousness in the book of Genesis is not the consciousness of its God character but the consciousness of its great writers, who include everything, and who don't see the opponent as the enemy. These writers have a generosity of spirit that always embraces the perspective of the unchosen, the defeated. There are no villains in the book; the unfavored brother can indeed, as in "The Meeting of Jacob and Esau," be portrayed as more sympathetic than the hero and morally superior to him. This generosity of spirit, which doesn't see people in terms of good and bad, us and them, is a rare and deeply admirable quality of mind that, as I worked on the translation, moved me more than I can say. It is a mark of spiritual maturity, and we find its radiant presence in J, in E, and in the Joseph author, as we find it in the *Iliad*, the other great ancient text that treats the opponent with princely impartiality. In this sense, Genesis is a book that is filled with God's own generosity.

Although there are many themes that run through the stories of the patriarchs, the central theme is the conflict between brothers.

This theme finds a magnificent resolution at the end of the Joseph story. But before it is resolved, there is another, more subtle resolution in "Judah and Tamar." If Joseph is the answer and mirror image to Cain, Judah is the mirror image to Adam.

One not wholly midrashic way of reading the Eden story is as a story about the consequences of blaming someone else for your mistake. If to the Lord's question Adam had answered, "Yes, I did eat the fruit," then he might still be in Paradise. But rather than taking responsibility, he turns the blame onto Eve, who turns it onto the serpent (who, not being asked, is too polite to point back to the Lord and thus complete the circle).

"Judah and Tamar" corrects Adam's failure. At the end of the story, Tamar, a woman of remarkable courage, shows Judah his pledge and says, "The man who got me pregnant is the owner of this seal and this staff; see if you recognize whose they are." And in the most dignified way, with the greatest forthrightness and integrity, Judah says, "She is in the right and I am in the wrong." It is as simple as that. In Judah's admission, both he and his daughter-in-law are healed. No explanations, no excuses; nothing further is necessary. There is no blame, not even self-blame.

Judah's acknowledgment is the mature adult response to a mistake, in contrast to Adam's childish shirking of responsibility. If Adam could have reacted with that kind of integrity, there would have been no split between his wife and him, and that oneness would have led to forgiveness, which leads to Paradise itself. Thus the second-to-last story in Genesis ends in a major chord that resolves the book's first dissonance (Adam and Eve), while the last story ends in an even greater major chord that resolves its second dissonance (Cain and Abel). For these connections, this sense of profound harmony, we should feel deeply grateful to R. Once we see them, we see the true shape of Genesis.

"Joseph and His Brothers," like *Job*, is a story of alienation and return. The Joseph author tells the same story in a different mode, narrative rather than metaphysical, with no grand vision at its climax. In fact, the very absence of God as a character in the Joseph story testifies to the spiritual insight of its author, whose motto, after all the shallow theophanies of the rest of Genesis, might be Job's next-to-last words turned upside down: "I had seen you with my eyes, / but now my ears have heard of you."

Joseph is the shaman of the tribe, the dreamer of visionary dreams, the son gifted with seemingly invulnerable charm, the image, in male form, of his father's only beloved wife. Here, once again, because the father's love is partial, it leads to disaster — apparent disaster. Joseph revels in the favoritism, unconscious of his brothers' jealousy, completely enclosed in his self-delight. In blurting out his dreams, he seems to be flaunting them in his brothers' faces, even in his father's face, as if he were saying, "Not only does Daddy love me best, God loves me best." But God doesn't accept the sweet smell of his offering; God is not that kind of god here; God is in the disaster. When the brothers throw Joseph into a pit and sell him, their action seems cruel but appropriate, a reaction to the imbalance in his own character. Joseph has to fall into darkness and slavery and great suffering, he has to learn a deeper humanity and become a clearer vessel of God than his favoredness has thus far permitted. He has to sit at the feet of his own suffering, the Buddha's first noble truth. There is a ferocious, compassionate intelligence at work here behind the scenes: the intelligence of the universe that we can appropriately call "God."

When we next hear Joseph talk about dreams, it is in prison, and it is about the dreams of others. He speaks with humility but with great confidence. His "I" has stepped out of the way. Now, rather than dreaming dreams, he can understand them. This leads directly, though with two more years' lag time, to his audience with Pharaoh and to his sudden, dreamlike advancement. Thus Joseph becomes the only character in Genesis to undergo a transformation into mastery, from the charming but arrogant brat of the beginning to the wise leader at the end. He arrives at such a depth of maturity that he can open his heart and completely forgive the brothers who almost murdered him. His compassion for them arises from his insight into the way things are, his profound and grateful understanding that, however desperate life may seem, there's a divinity that shapes our ends. When he reveals himself to his brothers in the great climactic scene, he reveals himself to us.

> Don't be troubled now, and don't blame yourselves for selling me, because God sent me ahead of you to save lives. For two years now the famine has gripped the land, and there will be five more years without a harvest. But God sent me ahead of you, and he has made me a father to Pharaoh, and master of all his household, and ruler over all Egypt. So it was not you but God who sent me here. [45:5-8]

"Joseph and His Brothers" is the resolution of the stories of Cain and his brother and Isaac and his brother and Jacob and his brother. The sins of the fathers and mothers are remedied in the forgiveness

of the son. But in its radiant, tearful, joyous climax, it is also a further resolution of the Eden story. Forgiveness is not only a return
to Eden but an entrance into a world that is deeper and more serene
than Adam and Eve's garden. It is the adult counterpart to the
unconscious happiness of childhood where all humans begin. It is a
sabbath of the heart.

NOTES TO "ON TRANSLATING GENESIS"

p. xi   *Do you have the patience to wait:* Stephen Mitchell, *Tao Te Ching: A New English Version,* HarperCollins, 1988, chapter 15.

p. xiv   *straightforward in its syntax:* Robert Alter calls J's (and E's) style "wonderfully compact, beautifully cadenced Hebrew, using a supple, predominantly paratactic syntax" (*The World of Biblical Literature,* Basic Books, 1992, p. 155). Whenever possible, I have kept this syntax in my English. And unlike most contemporary translators, I have kept the many *and*s of the Hebrew (except where *and* equalled *but* or *then*), since that is an essential quality of its storytelling style. "What is important . . . is not this word or that but the overall rhythm established by the simple conjunction 'and' (*wa*) . . . . Readers of the AV, as of the Hebrew, find themselves rocked into a mood both of acquiescence and of expectation, grasping 'what is going on' and assenting to it, long before they have understood precisely what this is" (Gabriel Josipovici, *The Book of God: A Response to the Bible,* Yale University Press, 1988, p. 60).

p. xv   *It has to be living, to learn the speech of the place:* Wallace Stevens, "Of Modern Poetry," in *The Collected Poems of Wallace Stevens,* Alfred A. Knopf, 1954, pp. 239f.

p. xvii   *the Lord had made:* The term *YHVH Elohim,* "Lord God" (literally, "YHVH God"), which is used only in this story, seems to have been created by an editor, not the original author (see the note to 2:4b, pp. 123f.). The other term usually translated "Lord God" is *Adonai YHVH* (literally, "Lord YHVH"); it occurs in 15:2,8 (pp. 27f.)

p. xvii   *and beautiful to look at:* I have omitted the third phrase, usually translated "the tree was desirable for acquiring wisdom," because it is probably a manuscript variant. See the note to 3:6, p. 124.

p. xxii   *whom you said you would bring to me:* See note to 43:29, p. 157.

p. xxiii   *the verse actually meant:* Actually, the first half of the verse is truncated in the Hebrew text. The verb, *'em'as,* means "to reject" or "to regard as of little value," never "to abhor or despise." Since the object has somehow dropped out of the text, it must be supplied by the translator. "Myself" is based on a misunderstanding of the verb. A sounder interpretation, first proposed in the ancient Syriac version, would be: "Therefore I take back (everything I said)." In the second half of the verse, the verb, as used in *Job*, always means "to comfort." The phrase *nihamti 'al* means "to be comforted about" or possibly "to repent of," but not "to repent in or upon." Nor does *'afar va-'efer* indicate the place where Job is sitting. This phrase, which occurs once before in *Job* and twice elsewhere in the Bible, always refers to the human body, which was created from dust and returns to dust. So the literal meaning is: "and I am comforted about (being) dust."

p. xxiv *16:6-7:* Chapter and verse numbers throughout this book are those of the Hebrew text, which occasionally differ from those of the standard English translations.

p. xxv *several hundred pita breads:* The Hebrew says "three *seahs* of our best flour," which has been estimated to equal approximately one bushel (sixty pounds of wheat flour): an extravagantly generous amount for three guests.

p. xxvi *indicates mental anguish:* As also in 1 Samuel 18:8 and Jonah 4:1,9.

p. xxxi *thirteen years old:* According to P's genealogy, Ishmael is fourteen when Isaac is born (16:16, 21:5). If the weaning (21:8) takes place at its customary time, when Isaac is three, Ishmael is seventeen at the time of this story.

p. xxxii *only of Ishmael and Joseph:* "And the Lord was with Joseph" (39:2). P's statements about Enoch and Noah, that they "walked with God," have a slightly different sense.

p. xxxvii *why do I live?:* The Hebrew phrase is obscure. For these two verses, see the note to 25:22-23, p. 140.

p. xxxviii *the Joseph story seems to be a unified whole:* R's most famous interruption is "Judah and Tamar," an independent story that he inserted after chapter 37. I have placed it before the Joseph story. Whatever interesting resonances it may have in its traditional place, it is inappropriate there, since the Judah of "Joseph and His Brothers" is a considerably younger man, who in chapter 43 is still living with his father and brothers.

p. xxxviii *"Joseph and His Brothers Reconciled":* Some readers find this story touching in spite of the clumsiness and bathos of its style, because it shows the brothers feeling guilty even after many years. In any case, this is a different story, with a different chronology, from the original author's, who has Joseph's forgiveness given and received once and completely. P states that Jacob lived in Egypt for seventeen years; in the original story he dies shortly after arriving in Egypt. Only according to this original chronology does Jacob's deathbed statement that "I thought I would never see you again, and now God has let me see your children too" make sense.

p. xxxix   ehyéh, "I am":

> And God said to Moses, "I am what I am." And he said, "This is what you should say to the Israelites: 'I am has sent me to you'" (Exodus 3:14).

p. xxxix   *There was something formless and perfect:* Tao Te Ching: A New English Version, chapter 25.

p. xli   *God does not command murder:* In "The Dispute between the Philosophical and Theological Faculties," Kant wrote, "There are some cases in which you can be absolutely certain that it is not God whose voice you hear; when the voice commands you to do what is opposed to the moral law, though the phenomenon may seem to you more majestic than the whole of nature, you must count it as a deception. The myth of the sacrifice of Abraham can serve as an example: Abraham, at God's command, was going to slaughter his own son — the poor child in his ignorance even carried the wood. Abraham should have said to this supposed divine voice: 'That I am not to kill my beloved son is quite certain; that you who appear to me are God, I am not certain, nor can I ever be, even if your voice thunders from the heavens.'"

p. xliv   In *the Beginning:* It is common in contemporary translations for the first three words of Genesis to be rendered "When God began to create . . ." But there are excellent reasons, both grammatical and substantive, to prefer the more familiar interpretation, which dates back to the Septuagint. See Westermann's exhaustive, meticulous exegesis of 1:1.

p. xliv   *great, methodical exuberance:* For a wonderful elaboration of P's account, see Book VII of Milton's *Paradise Lost.*

p. xlv   *he creates the serpent:* Christians later identified the serpent with Satan, but in J's story he is simply an animal (though a clever and persuasive one).

p. xlv   *Each in his own way is a truth-teller:* The serpent tells the truth when he

<INTRODUCTION>

says that Eve will not die when she eats the fruit, whereas the Lord's statement in 2:17 is plainly untrue. Interpreters sometimes fudge this point by supposing that what the Lord meant was "you will become mortal"—a meaning that the Hebrew phrase can't possibly have. But death was in the garden from the beginning. We know that Adam and Eve weren't created immortal because, as the Lord says in 3:22 (presumably to the other Elohim), the only way they can live forever is if they eat from the Tree of Life.

p. xlviii *Men are not punished* for . . . : Elbert Hubbard.

p. xlviii *as in "The Meeting of Jacob and Esau"*: When the brothers meet, Esau, who has been wronged, throws his arms around Jacob, bursts into tears of joy, and shows himself to be a much more openhearted character. Jacob remains rather shifty and calculating, stuck in the karma of his deceit.

p. xlix *both he and his daughter-in-law are healed*: The national importance of this story lay in a fact known by everyone: that Perez, one of the twins born from the union of Judah and Tamar, was the ancestor of King David. Thus, in Jewish and Christian terms, Judah's acknowledgment literally as well as metaphorically leads to the birth of the Messiah.

p. l *his father's only beloved wife*: Though he never mentions Rachel, the Joseph author implies that she is alive at the beginning of the story when he has Jacob say, "What is the meaning of this dream of yours? Do you really think that I and your mother and your brothers will come and bow down before you?"

The Book of
GENESIS

<1:1>

The Creation

ACCORDING TO *P*

In the beginning, God created the heavens and the earth. And the earth was chaos, and there was darkness over the abyss, and the spirit of God hovered upon the waters. And God said, "Let there be light." And there was light. And God saw that the light was good. And God separated the light from the darkness. And God called the light Day, and the darkness he called Night. And there was evening, and there was morning: a first day.

And God said, "Let there be a dome in the midst of the waters, to separate waters from waters." And it was so: God made the dome, and it separated the waters below it from the waters above it. And God saw that it was good. And God called the dome Sky. And there was evening, and there was morning: a second day.

And God said, "Let the waters below the sky gather into one place, and let the dry land appear." And it was so. And God called the dry land Earth, and the gathered waters he called Sea. And God saw that it was good. And God said, "Let the earth sprout with green things: plants that bear seeds, and every kind of tree that bears fruit with its seed in it." And it was so: the earth became green with plants and with every kind of fruit tree. And God saw that it was good. And there was evening, and there was morning: a third day.

< 1:14 >

And God said, "Let there be lights in the dome of the sky, to separate the day from the night. And let them shine on the earth, and mark the set times, the days and the years." And it was so: God made the two great lights — the greater one to rule the day, and the lesser one to rule the night — and also the stars. And God set them in the dome of the sky to shine on the earth, and to rule the day and the night, and to separate the light from the darkness. And God saw that it was good. And there was evening, and there was morning: a fourth day.

And God said, "Let the waters teem with living creatures, and let birds fly above the earth across the dome of the sky." And it was so: God created the great whales, and every kind of creature that the waters teem with, and every kind of bird. And God saw that it was good. And God blessed them, saying, "Be fruitful and multiply, and fill the waters of the sea, and let the birds multiply on the earth." And there was evening, and there was morning: a fifth day.

And God said, "Let the earth bring forth living things of all kinds — animals and reptiles and every kind of creature." And it was so: God made animals of all kinds, and every kind of reptile, and every kind of creature. And God saw that it was good. And God said, "Let us make humans, in our own image, similar to us; and let them rule over the fish of the sea and the birds of the sky and the animals and the reptiles and every creature on earth." And God created humans in his own image, in the image of God he created them, male and female he created them. And God blessed them and said to them, "Be fruitful and multiply, and fill the earth and govern it, and rule over the fish of the sea and the birds of the sky and every creature on earth." And God said, "Here: I give you every plant that

<1:29>

bears seeds and every tree that bears fruit; they will be your food. And to all the animals and to all the birds of the sky and to all creatures on earth, I give every green plant as their food." And God saw everything that he had made, and indeed it was very good. And there was evening, and there was morning: the sixth day.

Thus the heavens and the earth were completed, and everything in them. And on the seventh day God saw that his work was completed, and he rested on the seventh day from all the work that he had done. And God blessed the seventh day and made it holy, because on it he rested from all the work of creation.

The Creation

ACCORDING TO *J*

At the time when the Lord made earth and heaven — before there were any plants on the earth and before any grasses had sprouted, for the Lord had not sent rain on the earth and there was no one to work the ground, but a stream would well up from the earth to water the whole surface of the ground — the Lord formed a man from the dust of the ground and blew into his nostrils the breath of life, and the man became a living being.

And the Lord planted a garden in Eden, to the east, and he grew from the ground every kind of tree that is beautiful to look at and good to eat from, with the tree of life in the middle of the garden, and the tree of the knowledge of good and evil. And the Lord took the man he had formed and put him in the garden of Eden, to work it and care for it. And the Lord said to the man, "From all the trees

<2:16>

in the garden you are allowed to eat. But from the tree of the knowledge of good and evil you are not allowed to eat; for as soon as you eat from it, you will die."

And the Lord said, "It is not good for the man to be alone. I will make him a partner to help him." So from the ground the Lord formed all the animals and all the birds and brought each one to the man to see what he would call it. And whatever the man called it, that was its name. And the man gave names to all the birds and to all the animals; but for the man no partner was found.

So the Lord caused a deep trance to fall upon the man. And as the man slept, the Lord took out one of his ribs and closed up his side with flesh. And he built the rib into a woman, and he brought her to the man. And the man said, "This one at last is bone from my bone and flesh from my flesh. She will be called woman, because from man she was taken." (That is why a man leaves his father and mother and joins with his wife, and they become one flesh.) And both of them were naked, the man and his wife, and they felt no shame.

Now the serpent was more cunning than any creature the Lord had made. And he said to the woman, "Did God really say that you're not allowed to eat from any tree in the garden?"

And the woman said, "We *are* allowed to eat from any tree in the garden. It's just the tree in the middle of the garden that we must not eat from, because God said, 'If you eat from it, or even touch it, you die.'"

And the serpent said, "You will not die. God knows that as soon as you eat from it, your eyes will be opened, and you will be like gods, knowing good and evil."

<3:6>

7

And when the woman saw that the tree was good to eat from and beautiful to look at, she took one of its fruits and ate, and gave it to her husband, and he ate too. And the eyes of them both were opened, and they knew that they were naked. And they sewed fig leaves together and made loincloths for themselves.

And they heard the sound of the Lord walking in the garden in the cool of the day. And the man and his wife hid from the Lord among the trees of the garden.

And the Lord called to the man, "Where are you?"

And the man said, "I heard you walking in the garden, and I saw that I was naked, so I hid."

And the Lord said, "Who told you that you were naked? Have you eaten from the tree I commanded you not to eat from?"

And the man said, "The woman you gave me as a companion — she gave me a fruit from the tree, and I ate."

And the Lord said to the woman, "What is this that you have done!"

And the woman said, "The serpent tricked me, and I ate."

And the Lord said to the serpent,

> "Because you have done this,
>   cursed are you:
>   cut off from all the animals.
> On your belly you shall move
>   and dust you shall eat
>   all the days of your life.
> And I will put enmity
>   between you and the woman

<3:15>

and between your offspring and hers;
they shall strike at your head
and you shall strike at their heels."

And to the woman he said,

"I will greatly multiply
your suffering and your pain.
In pain you shall give birth to children;
and you shall be subject to your husband
and he shall rule over you."

And to the man he said, "Because you listened to your wife and ate from the tree I commanded you not to eat from,

Cursed is the ground beneath you;
thorns and thistles it shall sprout.
By the sweat of your face
you shall grow food,
until you return to the ground,
as you were taken from it.
For dust you are,
and to dust you shall return."

And the man named his wife Eve, *Life*, because she became the mother of all the living.

And the Lord made clothes of skin for the man and his wife, and dressed them.

And the Lord said, "Now that the man has become like one of us,

<3:22>

knowing good and evil, what if he reaches out and takes a fruit from the tree of life too, and eats, and lives forever?"

So the Lord drove him out of the garden of Eden, to work the ground he had been taken from. He banished the man, and at the east of the garden he stationed the kerubs and the fiery whirling sword, to guard the path to the tree of life.

Cain and Abel
J

The man had slept with his wife Eve, and she conceived and gave birth to Cain, *He Who Is Created*, and she said, "I have created a man, just as the Lord did!" And later she gave birth to his brother Abel. And Abel became a shepherd, and Cain a farmer.

After a while Cain brought the first fruits of his harvest as an offering to the Lord, and Abel brought the fattest pieces of the firstlings from his flock. And the Lord accepted Abel and his offering; but Cain and his offering he didn't accept. And Cain was very troubled, and his face fell.

And Cain said to his brother Abel, "Let's go for a walk." And when they were alone, Cain turned on his brother Abel and killed him.

And the Lord said to Cain, "Where is your brother Abel?"

And he said, "I don't know. Am I my brother's keeper?"

And the Lord said, "What have you done! Listen: your brother's blood is crying out to me from the ground. Now you are cursed: cut

<4:11>

off from the ground that opened to swallow your brother's blood. When you work the ground, it will no longer yield its strength to you. You will become a restless wanderer on the earth."

And Cain said, "My punishment is greater than I can bear. You have banished me from this land, and I must submit to you and become a restless wanderer on the earth, and anyone who meets me can kill me."

And the Lord said, "No: if anyone kills you, you will be avenged seven times over." And the Lord put a mark on Cain, to keep anyone who met him from killing him. And Cain went away from the Lord and settled in the land of Nod, *Restlessness*, east of Eden.

Seth; The Descendants of Cain
J

And Adam slept with his wife again, and she gave birth to a son, and named him Seth, *He Who Is Granted*, for she said, "God has granted me another child!" And Seth also had a son, and he named him Enosh. It was at this time that the Lord's name YHVH was first invoked.

And Cain slept with his wife, and she conceived and gave birth to Enoch. And Enoch built a city and named it after himself. And Enoch fathered Irad, and Irad fathered Mehujael, and Mehujael fathered Methushael, and Methushael fathered Lamech. And Lamech fathered a son and named him Noah, *He Who Brings Pleasure*, for he said, "Out of the ground that the Lord cursed, this one will bring us pleasure, after our work and the toil of our hands."

The Descendants of Lamech

J

And Lamech married two women: the name of the first was Adah and the name of the second was Zillah. And Adah gave birth to Jabal: he was the ancestor of those who live in tents and with livestock. And his brother's name was Jubal: he was the ancestor of those who play the lyre and the flute. And Zillah gave birth to Tubal: he was the ancestor of those who forge tools of copper and iron, and his sister was named Naamah. And Lamech said to his wives:

"Adah and Zillah, hear my voice;
    you wives of Lamech, listen to my words.
I have killed a man for wounding me,
    I have slain someone for harming me.
If Cain is avenged seven times,
    then Lamech seventy-seven times."

Genealogies [P]

This is the list of the descendants of Adam. When God created humans, he made them in the image of God; male and female he created them. And when they were created, he blessed them, and named them adam, *man*.

And when Adam was a hundred and thirty years old, he fathered a son in his own image, similar to him, and he named him Seth. And Adam lived another eight hundred years, and he fathered sons and daughters; and Adam died when he was nine hundred and thirty years old. And Seth was a hundred and five years old when he fathered Enosh; and he lived another eight hundred and seven years, and he fathered sons and daughters; and Seth died when he was nine hundred and twelve years old. And Enosh was ninety years old when he fathered Kenan; and he lived another eight hundred and fifteen years, and he fathered sons and daughters; and Enosh died when he was nine hundred and five years old. And Kenan was seventy years old when he fathered Mahalalel; and he lived another eight hundred and forty years, and he fathered sons and daughters; and Kenan died when he was nine hundred and ten years old. And Mahalalel was sixty-five years old when he fathered Jared; and he lived another eight hundred and thirty years, and he fathered sons and daughters; and Mahalalel died when he was eight hundred and ninety-five years old. And Jared was a hundred and sixty-two years old when he fathered Enoch; and he lived another eight hundred years, and he fathered sons and daughters; and Jared died when he was nine hundred and sixty-two years old. And Enoch was sixty-five years old when he fathered Methuselah. And Enoch walked with God. And he lived another three hundred years, and he fathered sons and daughters; and Enoch lived three hundred and sixty-five years. And Enoch walked with God, then he vanished, for God took him. And Methuselah was a hundred and eighty-seven years old when he fathered Lamech; and he lived another seven hundred and eighty-two years, and he fathered sons and daughters; and Methuselah died when he was nine hundred and sixty-nine years old. And Lamech was a hundred and eighty-two years old when he fathered Noah; and he lived another five hundred and ninety-five years, and he fathered sons and daughters; and Lamech died when he was seven hundred and seventy-seven years old. And Noah was five hundred years old when he fathered Shem, Ham, and Japheth.

The Gods and the Women

J

When humans began to multiply on the earth and women were born to them, the gods saw that the women were beautiful, and they took as wives any of them they wanted.

It was in those days that the giants appeared on the earth: when the gods slept with the women, and children were born to them. These were the heroes who lived long ago, the men of great fame.

The Flood

ACCORDING TO J

Now when the Lord saw how great the evil of humans was, and how every impulse in their hearts was nothing but evil all the time, he was sorry that he had made humans on the earth, and he was pained in his heart. And he said, "I will destroy all humankind from the earth: I am sorry I ever made them." But Noah found favor with the Lord.

And the Lord said to Noah, "Go into the ark, with all your household; for you alone I have found righteous in this age. Take with you seven pairs, male and female, of all the clean animals, and one pair, male and female, of all the unclean animals, to make sure that life continues on the earth. Seven days from now, I will make it rain on the earth for forty days and forty nights; and I will destroy from the earth every creature that I made." And Noah did as the Lord had commanded him.

And after seven days, the waters of the flood came onto the earth. And Noah, with all his household, went into the ark because of the great flood, and the Lord shut the door behind him. And the rain fell onto the earth for forty days and forty nights. And the waters rose and lifted the ark above the earth. And the Lord destroyed every creature on earth: everything that had the breath of life in its nostrils, everything on the dry land, died. And only Noah was left, and those who were with him in the ark.

And at the end of forty days the rain was held back from heaven, and the waters stopped rising above the earth. And Noah opened the window he had made in the ark, and he sent out a dove, to see if the waters had subsided. But the dove found no place where her feet could settle, because the waters still covered the whole earth, and she returned to the ark. And Noah put out his hand and took her and brought her into the ark.

And he waited seven more days. And again he sent out the dove from the ark. And toward evening the dove came back to him, and there in her beak was a freshly plucked olive leaf, and Noah knew that the waters had subsided.

And he waited seven more days. And he sent out the dove. And she didn't return.

And Noah took off the ark's cover and looked out, and indeed the ground was dry.

And Noah built an altar to the Lord, and he took one of every clean animal and bird and offered them as sacrifices on the altar. And the Lord smelled the soothing odor and said to himself, "Never again will I curse the ground because of humans, however evil the impulse of the human heart may be, and never again will I

15

strike down all living things as I have done. For as long as the earth endures, these will not end: seedtime and harvest, cold and heat, summer and winter, day and night."

The Flood

ACCORDING TO P

This is the story of Noah. Noah was a righteous man, the one blameless man in that age. Noah walked with God. And Noah had three sons: Shem, Ham, and Japheth.

And the earth was exceedingly corrupt and filled with violence. And when God saw how corrupt the earth was and how corrupt humankind had become on the earth, God said to Noah, "I am going to put an end to humankind, for the earth is filled with violence because of them: I am going to blot them out from the earth. Make yourself an ark of cypress wood; cover it with reeds and caulk it inside and outside with pitch. Make it with lower, second, and third decks. And this is how you should make it: the ark should be five hundred feet long, one hundred feet wide, and fifty feet high. Make a skylight for the ark, and finish it two feet from the top. And put an entrance to the ark in its longer side.

"I am going to bring a great flood onto the earth, to exterminate all living creatures: everything on earth will perish. But I promise to rescue you; you will go into the ark, you and your sons and your wife and your sons' wives with you. And you will take one pair of every kind of creature, male and female, into the ark to stay alive with you. One pair of every kind of bird, animal, and reptile will come to you, to stay alive. And you will take with you all the food that you need, and store it away, to serve as food for you and for them." And Noah did everything God had commanded.

And Noah was six hundred years old when the flood came onto the earth; in the six hundredth year of Noah's life, in the second month, on the seventeenth day of the month, all the wells of the great deep burst, and the floodgates of heaven opened. On that day Noah, and Shem, Ham, and Japheth, Noah's sons, and Noah's wife, and the three wives of his sons with them, went into the ark, and with them every kind of animal, reptile, and bird: one pair of every creature went into the ark with Noah, a male and a female, as God had commanded him.

And the flood came down onto the earth, and the waters rose higher above the earth, and the ark drifted on the waters. And the waters rose higher and higher above the earth, until they covered the highest mountains under heaven. Thirty feet above the mountains the waters rose. And all creatures on earth perished—all birds and all animals and all reptiles and all humans.

And when the waters had risen above the earth for a hundred and fifty days, God remembered Noah and all the creatures that were with him in the ark, and the wells of the deep and the floodgates of heaven were shut. And God swept a wind over the earth, and the waters stopped rising. And at the end of the hundred and fifty days the waters began to subside. And in the seventh month, on the seventeenth day of the month, the ark came to rest on the mountains of Ararat. And the waters kept subsiding until the tenth month: in the tenth month, on the first day of the month, the tops of the mountains appeared.

And in the six hundred and first year, in the first month, on the first day of the month, the waters began to dry from the earth. And in the second month, on the twenty-seventh day of the month, the earth was dry.

And God said to Noah, "Come out of the ark, you and your wife and your sons and your sons' wives with you. And bring out every creature that is with you, every bird, animal, and reptile, and let them be fruitful and multiply and spread over all the earth."

And Noah came out, and his sons and his wife and his sons' wives with him. And every creature, every animal, bird, and reptile, group by group, came out of the ark.

And God blessed Noah and his sons, saying, "Be fruitful and multiply, and replenish the earth. And the fear of you will fall on every animal, every bird, every creature on earth, and every fish in the sea: they are all in your power. Every creature that moves will be yours to eat; I give them all to you, just as I gave you the green plants. But you must not eat flesh from a still-living animal. And I will require an accounting for the death of every human: I will require it from every animal, and I will require it from every human. Whoever sheds human blood, his blood will be shed; for in his own image did God make humans."

And God said to Noah and to his sons, "For your part, be fruitful and multiply; spread over the earth and rule it. For my part, I now make a solemn promise to you and to your offspring after you and to every creature that was with you, all birds and animals and reptiles that came out of the ark. And I will keep my promise to you: never again will all creatures be destroyed by the waters of a flood, and never again will there be a flood to blot out the earth."

And God said, "This is the sign of the promise that I make to you and to every creature that was with you, for all ages to come: I am setting my rainbow in the clouds, and it will be the sign of my promise to the earth. And whenever I bring clouds over the earth and the rainbow appears in the clouds, I will remember my promise to you and to every creature, and the waters will never again become a flood to blot out all life. And when the rainbow appears in the clouds, I will see it and remember the eternal promise I have made to every creature on earth."

Noah's Drunkenness

J

Now the sons of Noah who came out of the ark were Shem, Ham, and Japheth, and from them the whole earth was peopled.

And Noah was the first man to plant a vineyard. And he drank the wine and got drunk and lay naked inside his tent. And Ham, the father of Canaan, saw his father's genitals and went out and told his brothers. And Shem and Japheth took a robe and put it over their shoulders and walked in backward and covered their father's genitals; and they kept looking the other way and didn't see their father's genitals.

And when Noah was sober and found out what his youngest son had done to him, he said, "Cursed be Canaan; may he be the lowest of slaves to his brothers." And he said, "May the Lord bless the tents of Shem, and may Canaan be his slave. May God enlarge Japheth so that he lives in the tents of Shem, and may Canaan be his slave."

Genealogies *[P, J]*

And Noah lived three hundred and fifty years after the flood. And he died when he was nine hundred and fifty years old.

These are the descendants of the sons of Noah — Shem, Ham, and Japheth — and of the sons who were born to them after the flood. The sons of Japheth are Gomer, Magog, Madai, Javan, Tubal, Meshech, and Tiras. And the sons of Gomer are Ashkenaz, Riphath, and Togarmah. And the sons of Javan are Elishah, Tarshish, the Kittites, and the Rodanites; from them the nations of the coastland spread out. These are the sons of Japheth, by their clans and languages, by their countries and their nations.

And the sons of Ham are Cush, Egypt, Put, and Canaan. And the sons of Cush are Seba, Havilah, Sabtah, Raamah, and Sabteca. And the sons of Raamah are Sheba and Dedan. And Cush fathered Nimrod, who was the first great conqueror on earth. He was a mighty hunter; hence the saying "Like Nimrod the mighty hunter." And the main cities of his kingdom were Babel, Erech, and Accad, all of them in Shinar. From that country he went into Assyria and built the great city of Nineveh and its suburbs, and also Calah, and Resen, which is between Nineveh and Calah. And Egypt fathered the Ludites, the Anamites, the Lehavites, the Naphtuhites, the Pathrusites, the Casluhites, and the Caphtorites, from whom the Philistines descended. And Canaan fathered Sidon, his firstborn, and Heth; and the Jebusites, the Amorites, the Girgashites, the Hivites, the Arkites, the Sinites, the Arvadites, the Zemarites, and the Hamathites. (Afterward the clans of the Canaanites spread out, and their territory extended from Sidon toward Gerar, as far as Gaza, and toward Sodom, Gomorrah, Admah, and Zeboyim, as far as Lasha.) These are the sons of Ham, by their clans and languages, in their countries and their nations.

And Shem also had sons; he was the father of all the sons of

<10:21>

Eber, and the elder brother of Japheth. The sons of Shem are Elam, Asshur, Arpachshad, Lud, and Aram. And the sons of Aram are Uz, Hul, Gether, and Mash. And Arpachshad fathered Shelah; and Shelah fathered Eber. And Eber had two sons: the name of the first was Peleg, *Division*, because in that age the inhabitants of the earth were divided; and his brother's name was Joktan. And Joktan fathered Almodad, Sheleph, Hazarmaveth, Jerah, Hadoram, Uzal, Diklah, Obal, Abimael, Sheba, Ophir, Havilah, and Jobab: all these were the sons of Joktan. And their settlements extended from Mesha toward Sephar, as far as the hill country to the east. These are the sons of Shem, by their clans and languages, in their countries and their nations.

These are the clans of the sons of Noah, according to their origins, by their nations. And from them the nations spread out over the earth after the flood.

The Tower of Babel

J

At that time everyone on earth spoke one language. And as they traveled from the east, they arrived at a valley in Shinar and settled there. And they said to one another, "Come, let us build a city and a tower whose top will reach the sky; and let us provide for ourselves there, so that we will not be scattered over all the earth." And they said, "Come, let us make bricks and bake them hard." (Bricks were their stones, and asphalt their mortar.)

And the Lord saw the city and the tower that the humans were building. And he said, "If this is how they have begun to act, while they are one people and they all have one language, nothing they wish for will be beyond their reach. Come, let us go down and make a babble of their language, so that no one will understand what anyone else is saying."

So they stopped building the city, and the Lord scattered them over all the earth. That is why the city is named Babel, because it was there that the Lord made a babble of the language of all the earth, and from there he scattered them over all the earth.

Genealogies [P]

These are the descendants of Shem. Shem was a hundred years old when he fathered Arpachshad, two years after the flood; and he lived another five hundred years, and he fathered sons and daughters. And Arpachshad was thirty-five years old when he fathered Shelah; and he lived another four hundred and three years, and he fathered sons and daughters. And Shelah was thirty years old when he fathered Eber; and he lived another four hundred and three years, and he fathered sons and daughters. And Eber was thirty-four years old when he fathered Peleg; and he lived another four hundred and thirty years, and he fathered sons and daughters. And Peleg was thirty years old when he fathered Reu; and he lived another two hundred and nine years, and he fathered sons and daughters. And Reu was thirty-two years old when he fathered Serug; and he lived another two hundred and seven years, and he fathered sons and daughters. And Serug was thirty years old when he fathered Nahor; and he lived another two hundred years, and he fathered sons and daughters. And Nahor was twenty-nine years old when he fathered Terah; and he lived another hundred and nineteen years, and he fathered sons and daughters. And Terah was seventy years old when he fathered Abram, Nahor, and Haran.

<11:27>

These are the descendants of Terah: Terah fathered Abram, Nahor, and Haran; and Haran fathered Lot. And Haran died before his father Terah did, in his native land, Ur of the Chaldeans. And Abram and Nahor took wives: the name of Abram's wife was Sarai, and the name of Nahor's wife was Milcah, daughter of Haran and sister of Iscah. And Sarai was barren; she had no children. And Terah took his son Abram, and Lot, the son of Haran, and Sarai his daughter-in-law, and they left Ur of the Chaldeans and set out for Canaan; but when they came to Haran, they settled there. And Terah died in Haran when he was two hundred and five years old.

The Promise to Abram

J

And the Lord said to Abram, "Leave your native land and your family and your father's house, and go to the land that I will show you. And I will make you into a great nation, and I will bless you and make your name great, and you will be a blessing. And I will bless those who bless you, and curse those who curse you; and in you all the peoples of the earth will be blessed."

And Abram went, as the Lord had told him to; and Lot went with him. And they arrived in Canaan and passed through the land as far as the sanctuary at Shechem, the great oak of Moreh. (The Canaanites were then in the land.)

And the Lord appeared to Abram and said, "I give this land to your descendants." And Abram built an altar to the Lord there. And from there he moved on to the hill country east of Beth-El and

<12:8>

pitched his tent between Beth-El to the west and Ai to the east. And he built an altar to the Lord there, and he invoked the Lord's name. And Abram traveled on, by stages, toward the Negev.

Wife and Sister

VERSION I: J

And there was a famine in the land. And Abram went down to Egypt to stay for a while, because the famine was severe. And as he was about to enter Egypt, he said to Sarai, "Listen to me now: you are a beautiful woman; when the Egyptians see you and find out that you are my wife, they will kill me. So tell them that you are my sister, and I will be treated well for your sake, and they will spare my life because of you."

And indeed when Abram came into Egypt, the Egyptians saw that the woman was very beautiful. And Pharaoh's courtiers saw her and praised her to Pharaoh; and she was taken into Pharaoh's household. And he treated Abram well for her sake, and gave him sheep, oxen, donkeys, male and female slaves, and camels.

But the Lord afflicted Pharaoh with great plagues because of Sarai. And Pharaoh summoned Abram and said, "What have you done to me! Why didn't you tell me that she was your wife? Why did you say she was your sister, so that I took her as a wife? Here she is now: take her and go." And Pharaoh put men in charge of him, and they took him to the border, with his wife and all his possessions.

Abram and Lot

J

And Abram went up out of Egypt into the Negev, with his wife and everything he owned; and Lot went with him. And Abram was very rich in livestock, silver, and gold. And he traveled by stages from the Negev to the place between Beth-El and Ai where he had pitched his tent before, where he had built an altar and invoked the Lord's name.

And Lot too had many sheep, oxen, and camels. And there was quarreling between Abram's herdsmen and Lot's. (The Canaanites and the Perizzites were still living in the land at that time.) And Abram said to Lot, "Since we are kinsmen, let us have no conflict between you and me, or between your people and mine. Isn't the whole country open for you to live in? So please go your own way: if you go left, I will go right; if you go right, I will go left."

And Lot looked around and saw that the whole plain of the Jordan was well watered, all the way to Zoar, like the garden of the Lord, like the land of Egypt (this was before the Lord destroyed Sodom and Gomorrah). So Lot chose the whole plain of the Jordan, and he traveled east and pitched his tent near Sodom.

And after Lot had departed, the Lord said to Abram, "Look around now, north, south, east, and west: all the land that you see, I give to you and to your descendants for all time. And I will make your descendants as numberless as the dust of the earth: if anyone could count up the dust of the earth, then your descendants could

<13:16>

be counted. Get up now and walk through the land, through the length and breadth of it: I give it to you."

Then Abram moved his tent and settled in Hebron, by the great oaks of Mamre, and built an altar to the Lord there.

Abram and the Kings

LATE REDACTOR, USING THREE EARLY SOURCES

When Amraphel king of Babylon, Arioch king of Ellasar, Chedorlaomer king of Elam, and Tidal king of Goyim went to war against Bera king of Sodom, Birsha king of Gomorrah, Shinab king of Admah, Shemeber king of Zeboyim, and the king of Bela (which is now Zoar), all these joined forces and proceeded to the valley of Siddim (which is now the Dead Sea). For twelve years they had been vassals to Chedorlaomer, but in the thirteenth year they rebelled. Then in the fourteenth year Chedorlaomer and the kings who were allied with him came and defeated the Rephaites at Ashteroth-karnayim, the Zuzites at Ham, the Emites at Shaveh-kiryatayim, and the Horites in the hill country of Seir, as far as El-paran, on the edge of the wilderness. Then they turned back and went to En-mishpat (which is now Kadesh) and conquered all the territory of the Amalekites and of the Amorites who lived in Hazazon-tamar. Then the king of Sodom, the king of Gomorrah, the king of Admah, the king of Zeboyim, and the king of Bela marched out to the valley of Siddim and joined battle against them — against Chedorlaomer king of Elam, Tidal king of Goyim,

Amraphel king of Babylon, and Arioch king of Ellasar: four kings against five. Now the valley of Siddim was full of asphalt pits, and the kings of Sodom and Gomorrah fled and climbed down into them and hid, and the others fled to the hill country. And the four kings took all the livestock of Sodom and Gomorrah and all their provisions, and they went away.

And they also took Lot and his livestock — Abram's brother's son — and they went away (he was living in Sodom). And one of the survivors went and told Abram the Hebrew, who had settled by the great oaks of Mamre the Amorite, kinsman of Eshcol and of Aner, who were allies of Abram. And when Abram heard that his kinsman Lot had been taken captive, he called up his retainers, his own slaves, three hundred and eighteen of them, and followed them northward to Dan. And he divided his men into groups and attacked them by night and defeated them and pursued them as far as Hobah, north of Damascus. And he recovered all the livestock, and also his kinsman Lot and his livestock, and the women and the captives. And after Abram returned from defeating Chedorlaomer and the kings who were allied with him, the king of Sodom came out to meet him in the valley of Shaveh (which is now the Valley of the King).

And Melchizedek king of Salem brought out bread and wine; he was a priest of Almighty God. And he blessed him, saying, "Blessed be Abram by Almighty God, creator of heaven and earth. And blessed be Almighty God, who delivered your enemies into your power." And Abram gave him a tenth of everything he had captured.

And the king of Sodom said to Abram, "Give me the people and take the livestock for yourself."

<14:22>

And Abram said, "I swear to the Lord, Almighty God, creator of heaven and earth, that I will not take even a thread or a sandal strap of what is yours, so that you can never say, 'I am the one who made Abram rich.' I will take just what my men have used up, and the share of my allies, Aner, Eshcol, and Mamre; they are entitled to their share."

The Promise to Abram: Descendants

LATE SOURCE

Some time later, the word of the Lord came to Abram in a vision and said, "Don't be afraid, Abram. I will give you a very great reward."

And Abram said, "Lord God, what reward can console me, since I will die childless and one of my slaves will be my heir?"

And the word of the Lord said, "That is not so: a son from your own loins will be your heir."

And he took him outside and said, "Look up now at the sky and count the stars if you can. So uncountable will your descendants be."

And Abram trusted the Lord; and the Lord regarded it to his merit.

<15:7>

The Promise to Abram: Land

LATE SOURCE

And the Lord said to Abram, "I am the Lord, who brought you out from Ur of the Chaldeans to give you this land as your possession."

And he said, "Lord God, how can I know that I will possess it?"

And he said, "Bring me a choice heifer, a choice she-goat, a choice ram, a dove, and a young pigeon."

And he brought him all these; and he split them down the middle, and laid each half opposite the other; but he didn't split the birds. And when vultures flew down onto the carcasses, Abram drove them away. And as the sun was setting, a deep trance fell upon Abram, and a great dread fell upon him. And when the sun had set and it was pitch-dark, a smoking firepot and a blazing torch passed between those pieces.

On that day the Lord made a promise to Abram: "I give this land to your descendants, from the river of Egypt to the river Euphrates."

Hagar and Ishmael

ACCORDING TO J

Now Sarai had not borne Abram any children. And she had an Egyptian maid whose name was Hagar. And Sarai said to Abram, "See how the Lord has prevented me from bearing children. I beg

<16:2>

you now, go and sleep with my maid, and perhaps I will have a son through her."

And Abram did what Sarai had asked: he slept with Hagar, and she conceived. And when she knew that she was pregnant, she began to look down on her mistress. And Sarai said to Abram, "It is your fault, this insult. I put my maid in your bed, and now that she is pregnant she looks down on me. May the Lord judge if I am right or not."

And Abram said, "Look, she is your maid; do what you want with her."

And Sarai treated her harshly, and she ran away. And the Lord found her near a spring in the wilderness, the spring on the way to Shur. And he said, "Hagar, where have you come from and where are you going?"

And she said, "I am running away from Sarai, my mistress."

And the Lord said to her, "You are pregnant, and you will give birth to a son, and you will name him Ishmael, *God Has Heard*, because the Lord has heard your suffering. And he will be a wild donkey, his hand against everyone, and everyone's hand against him; and he will live at odds with all his kinsmen."

And she called the Lord who had spoken to her El-ro'i, *A God Who Can Be Seen*; for she said, "Truly I have seen God and remained alive." That is why the well is named Beer-lahai-ro'i, *The Well of the One Who Saw and Remained Alive*; it is between Kadesh and Bered.

The Covenant with Abraham

P

And when Abram was ninety-nine years old, God appeared to him and said, "I am God Almighty; walk in my paths, and be blameless. And I will make a covenant between me and you, and I will multiply you very greatly."

And Abram prostrated himself on the ground. And God said to him, "For my part, this is my covenant with you: you will be the father of a multitude of nations. And your name will no longer be Abram, *Exalted Father*, but Abraham, *Father of a Multitude*; for I will make you the father of a multitude of nations. And I will make you very greatly fruitful, and will bring nations from you, and kings will come out of you. And I will keep my covenant with you and your descendants after you for all generations, as an everlasting covenant, that I will be your God and your descendants' God. And I will give you and your descendants after you the land that you are living in, the whole land of Canaan, as an everlasting possession, and I will be their God."

And God said to Abraham, "For your part, you will keep my covenant, you and your descendants after you for all generations. And this is how you will keep the covenant between me and you and your descendants after you: every male among you must be circumcised. You must circumcise the flesh of your foreskins, and that will be the sign of the covenant between me and you; at the age of eight days every male among you must be circumcised, throughout the generations. Even your slaves must be circumcised, whether

<17:12>

they are born in your household or bought with your money from a foreigner. Thus my covenant will be marked in your flesh as an everlasting covenant. And if any male does not have the flesh of his foreskin circumcised, he must be cut off from his people: he has broken my covenant."

And God said to Abraham, "As for Sarai your wife, you must no longer call her Sarai, but Sarah, *Princess*. And I will bless her and give you a son by her. I will bless her so that she gives rise to nations, and kings will issue from her."

And as Abraham lay prostrate on the ground, he laughed to himself and thought, "How can a son be born to a man who is a hundred years old? And how can a woman who is ninety years old bear a child?" And Abraham said to God, "May Ishmael too live in your favor."

And God said, "Sarah will indeed bear you a son; and you must name him Isaac, *He Laughs*. And I will keep my covenant with him as an everlasting covenant, and with his descendants after him. And as for Ishmael, *God Has Heard*, I have indeed heard you: I will bless him and make him fruitful, and will multiply him very greatly. He will father twelve chieftains, and I will make him into a great nation. But I will keep my covenant with Isaac, whom Sarah will bear to you at this season next year." And as soon as he had finished speaking with him, God vanished.

And Abraham took his son Ishmael and every male in his household, all the slaves born in his household or bought with his money, and he circumcised the flesh of their foreskins that very day, as God had told him to. And Abraham was ninety-nine years old when he circumcised the flesh of his foreskin, and Ishmael was thirteen.

Thus Abraham was circumcised on that very day, and his son Ishmael and all his male slaves, whether born in his household or bought with money from a foreigner, were circumcised along with him.

Abraham and the Three Visitors

J

And the Lord appeared to Abraham by the great oaks of Mamre as he sat before his tent in the heat of the day. And he looked up and saw three beings standing near him. And when he saw them, he ran from the tent to meet them, and he bowed to the ground and said, "Please, gentlemen, if I may ask you this favor, don't go on past me. Let me bring a little water for you to wash your feet, and you can stretch out under the tree. And I will send for a bit of bread, so that you can refresh yourselves now that you are here with me. And then you can continue on your way."

And they said, "All right, if it is no trouble."

And Abraham hurried into the tent and said to Sarah, "Hurry, take a bushel of our best flour, knead it, and bake pita." And Abraham ran to the herd, took a fine, plump calf, and gave it to a herdboy, who hurried to prepare it. And he took yogurt and milk and the calf that was now ready, and set it all before them; and he stood by them under the tree as they ate.

And they said to him, "Where is your wife, Sarah?"

And he said, "There, in the tent."

And one of them said, "I will return to you in nine months, and Sarah will have a son."

And Sarah had been listening at the entrance to the tent, behind him. (Abraham and Sarah were very old, and Sarah had long since stopped having periods.) And she laughed to herself and thought, "Withered as I am, can I be moist with pleasure, and my husband so old too?"

And the Lord said to Abraham, "Why did Sarah laugh and think she is too old to bear a child? Is anything too marvelous for the Lord? I will indeed return to you in nine months, and Sarah will have a son."

And Sarah lied and said, "I didn't laugh," because she was afraid.

And the Lord said, "Yes you did."

Abraham Questions the Destruction of Sodom

LATE SOURCE

Then the beings stood up and set out toward Sodom, and Abraham walked with them to see them off. And the Lord said to himself, "Should I hide from Abraham what I am about to do, since Abraham will become a great nation, and all the nations of the earth will be blessed in him? No: I will tell him, so that he may instruct his sons and his descendants to act as the Lord wishes, to do what is right and just, so that I may fulfill for him what I have promised."

<18:22>

And two of the beings turned and went down toward Sodom, but the Lord remained standing before Abraham. And the Lord said, "Because the outcry of Sodom and Gomorrah is so loud, I am going there myself, to see if their sin is as grave as it seems to be."

And Abraham stepped forward and said, "Will you destroy the innocent along with the guilty? What if there are fifty innocent men in the city: will you really destroy it, and not spare it for the sake of the fifty innocent men? It would be unworthy of you to kill the innocent along with the guilty, so that the innocent are punished like the guilty. That would be unworthy of you. Will the judge of the whole earth act unjustly?"

And the Lord said, "If I find fifty innocent men in Sodom, I will spare the whole city for their sake."

And Abraham said, "Forgive me if I dare to speak to the Lord, I who am merely dust. But what if five of the fifty innocent men are lacking? Will you destroy the whole city because of those five?"

And he said, "I will not destroy it if I find forty-five there."

And he said, "What if only forty are found?"

And he said, "I will not destroy it, for the sake of those forty."

And he said, "Please don't be angry if I speak again. What if only thirty are found?"

And he said, "I will not destroy it if I find thirty."

And he said, "Forgive me if I dare to speak to the Lord once more. What if only twenty are found?"

And he said, "I will not destroy it, for the sake of those twenty."

And he said, "Please don't be angry if I speak just one more time. What if ten are found?"

<18:32>

And he said, "I will not destroy it, for the sake of those ten."

And as soon as he had finished speaking with Abraham, the Lord went away. And Abraham returned to his home.

The Destruction of Sodom and Gomorrah

J

And the two beings came to Sodom in the evening, as Lot sat before the city gate. And when he saw them, he went up to them and made a deep bow. And he said, "Please, gentlemen, spend the night at my house, and wash your feet, and in the morning you can continue on your way."

And they said, "No, we will spend the night in the square."

But he kept pressing them until they agreed to go to his house. And when they got there, he made them a meal, and baked unleavened bread, and they ate.

Before they had gone to bed, the men of Sodom surrounded the house, young and old, down to the last man. And they called out to Lot, "Where are the men who came to you tonight? Bring them out here, so we can sleep with them."

And Lot went out into the entrance and shut the door behind him. And he said, "Friends, I beg you, don't do this wicked thing. Look, I have two daughters who have never slept with a man. Let me bring them out, and you can do whatever you want to them. But

<19:8>

don't do anything to these men, because they have come under the shelter of my roof."

And someone said, "Out of our way!" And someone said, "This fellow just got here, and now he is telling us what to do! Watch out, or you'll get it even worse than them!" And they pressed hard against Lot and moved in closer, to break down the door. But the beings reached out and pulled Lot inside and shut the door. And they struck the men at the entrance with a dazzling light, so that no one could find the door.

And the beings said to Lot, "Everyone in your family—your sons or daughters or anyone else—take them out of this place, because its outcry is so loud that the Lord has sent us to destroy it."

And Lot went out and said to his sons-in-law, "Hurry, get out of this place: the Lord is about to destroy it." But his sons-in-law thought he was joking.

And as soon as dawn came, the beings said to Lot, "Hurry, take your wife and the two daughters who are here, or you will be crushed in the punishment of the city." And he still lingered. And the beings took him by the hand, and his wife and the two daughters also, since the Lord was merciful to him, and they led them out and left them outside the city. And one of them said, "Run for your lives! Don't look back, don't stop anywhere on the plain: run to the hills or you will be crushed!"

And the Lord rained sulfurous fire on Sodom and Gomorrah, and he obliterated those cities, and the whole plain, and all the cities' inhabitants, and everything that grew on the ground.

And Lot's wife looked back, and she turned into a pillar of salt.

And in the morning Abraham went back to the place where he

<19:27>

had stood in the Lord's presence. And he looked down toward Sodom and Gomorrah, across the whole plain, and the smoke from it was rising like the smoke from a furnace.

Lot's Daughters
J

And Lot lived in a cave, with his two daughters.

And the elder one said to the younger, "Our father is old, and there are no men left on earth to sleep with us. Let's get him drunk with wine and sleep with him, so that life can be preserved through our father." And they got their father drunk that night. And the elder one went in and slept with her father, and he was not aware of when she lay down or of when she got up.

And the next day the elder one said to the younger, "Last night I slept with our father. Let's get him drunk again tonight, then you go in and sleep with him, so that life can be preserved through our father." And they got their father drunk that night as well. And the younger one went in and slept with her father, and he was not aware of when she lay down or of when she got up.

Thus both Lot's daughters became pregnant by their father. And the elder one gave birth to a son and named him Moab, *From Father*; he is the ancestor of the Moabites of today. And the younger one also gave birth to a son and named him Ben-ammi, *Son of My Kinsman*; he is the ancestor of the Ammonites of today.

<20:1>

Wife and Sister

VERSION 2: E

And Abraham traveled on toward the Negev, and settled between Kadesh and Shur. And while he was staying in Gerar, he told people that Sarah, his wife, was his sister. And Abimelech, king of Gerar, had Sarah brought to him. But God came to Abimelech in a dream one night and said, "You are a dead man: the woman you have taken is a married woman."

Now Abimelech had not slept with her, and he said, "My Lord, will you kill a man even though he is innocent? Didn't he tell me that she was his sister, and didn't she say it too? I did this with clean hands and a blameless heart."

And God said to him in the dream, "I know that you did this with a blameless heart; it was I who made you incapable of sleeping with her and thus kept you from sinning against me. But now you must return this man's wife; he is a prophet and will pray for you, and you will recover. But if you don't return her, know that you will die — you and all your household."

And the next morning Abimelech summoned his officials and told them what had happened. And they all were very frightened. And Abimelech summoned Abraham and said to him, "Why did you do this to us? What harm have I ever done you, to make you bring this great sin on me and my kingdom?"

And Abraham said, "I did it because I thought that there was no fear of God in this place, and that people would kill me because of my wife. And besides, she *is* my sister — my father's daughter, though not my mother's. And when God sent me out from my father's house, I said to her, 'Do this for me as a loyal wife: wherever we go, tell people that I am your brother.'"

And Abimelech took sheep and oxen and male and female slaves, and gave them to Abraham, and returned Sarah to him. And Abimelech said, "Look, my whole country is open for you to live in; you may settle wherever you wish." And to Sarah he said, "I have given your brother a thousand pieces of silver, to compensate you for everything that has happened and to prove that your honor has not been stained."

And Abraham prayed to God, and God healed Abimelech.

The Family of Abraham [P, R, *late source*]

And God did for Sarah as he had spoken, at the set time that God had told him of. And Abraham named his newborn son, whom Sarah had borne to him, Isaac. And when Isaac was eight days old, Abraham circumcised him, as God had commanded him. And Abraham was a hundred years old when his son Isaac was born.

Some time later, Abraham was told that Milcah too had borne sons to his brother Nahor: Uz the firstborn, his brother Buz, and Kemuel, the father of Aram, and Chesed, Hazo, Pildash, Jidlaph, and Bethuel. These eight Milcah bore to Nahor, Abraham's brother. And his concubine, whose name was Reumah, also bore sons: Tebah, Gaham, Tahash, and Maacah.

And Abraham took another wife, whose name was Keturah. And she bore him Zimran, Jokshan, Medan, Midian, Ishbak, and

Shuah. And Jokshan fathered Sheba and Dedan. And the descendants of Dedan became the Asshurites, the Letushites, and the Leummites. And the sons of Midian were Ephah, Epher, Enoch, Abida, and Eldaah. All these were the descendants of Keturah.

Hagar and Ishmael
ACCORDING TO E

And God provided for Sarah as he had promised, and Sarah conceived, and she bore Abraham a son in his old age. And Sarah named him Isaac, *He Laughs*, for she said, "God has brought me laughter; everyone who hears of this will laugh with me."

And the child grew, and on the day of his weaning Abraham gave a great feast. And Sarah saw the son of Hagar the Egyptian, whom she had borne to Abraham, playing with her son Isaac. And she said to Abraham, "Banish that slave and her son. I will not let the son of that slave share the inheritance with my son Isaac." And this troubled Abraham very greatly, because Ishmael too was his son.

And God said to Abraham, "Don't be troubled about the boy or about your slave. Do whatever Sarah tells you to, because it is through Isaac that your name will live on. As for the son of the slave, I will make him too into a great nation, because he is your child."

And in the morning, Abraham took food and a full waterskin, and gave them to Hagar, and put the child over her shoulder, and sent her away. And she wandered in the wilderness of Beer-sheba. And when the water in the skin was gone, she left the child under one of the bushes, and she went and sat down at a distance, about a bowshot away, for she thought, "How can I watch the child die?" And she sat there as he wailed.

And God heard the boy's cry, and he called to Hagar from heaven and said, "What is wrong, Hagar? Don't be afraid: *God has heard* the boy in his distress. Get up now, take him in your arms and encourage him; for I will make him into a great nation." And God opened her eyes, and she saw a well of water. And she went and filled the waterskin, and gave the boy a drink.

And God was with the boy as he grew up. And he lived in the wilderness of Paran and became an archer. And his mother found him a wife from Egypt.

Beer-sheba

VERSION 1: *E*

At about that time Abimelech said to Abraham, "God is with you in everything you do. Swear to me now by God that you will not act dishonestly with me or with my descendants and that, as I have been loyal to you, you will be loyal to me and to the people of the land where you have been living."

And Abraham said, "I swear it."

And Abraham took sheep and oxen and gave them to Abimelech, and the two of them made a pact. That is why that place was named Beer-sheba, *The Well of the Oath*, because the two of them swore an oath there.

Beer-sheba

VERSION 2: *J*

And Abraham complained to Abimelech about a well that Abimelech's men had seized. And Abimelech said, "I don't know who did this. You never told me, and this is the first time I have heard of it."

And Abraham set apart seven ewes from his flock. And Abimelech said, "What does this mean?"

And Abraham said, "Accept these seven ewes from me as proof that I am the one who dug this well." That is why that place was named Beer-sheba, *The Well of the Seven.*

The Binding of Isaac
E

Some time later, God tested Abraham. And he said to him, "Abraham."

And he said, "Yes."

And he said, "Take your son, your darling, whom you love, Isaac, and go to the land of Moriah, and burn him there as a sacrifice on one of the hills that I will show you."

And early in the morning Abraham saddled his donkey, and took two of his men with him, and his son Isaac, and the wood that he had chopped for the sacrifice, and set out for the place that God had spoken of.

On the third day, Abraham looked up and saw the place in the distance. And he said to his men, "You stay here with the donkey; I and the boy will go up there and worship and come back to you."

And Abraham took the wood for the sacrifice and put it on his son Isaac. And he himself took the firestone and the knife. And the two of them walked on together.

And Isaac said to his father Abraham, "Father."

And he said, "Yes, my son."

And he said, "Here are the firestone and the wood. But where is the sheep for the sacrifice?"

And Abraham said, "God will provide a sheep for the sacrifice, my son."

And the two of them walked on together.

And they came to the place that God had shown him. And Abraham built an altar there, and arranged the wood, and bound his son Isaac, and laid him on the altar, on top of the wood. And Abraham reached out and picked up the knife to slaughter his son.

And God called to him from heaven and said, "Abraham! Abraham!"

And he said, "Yes."

And he said, "Don't lay your hand on the boy or do him any harm. Now I know how deeply you revere God, since you have not withheld your son, your darling, from me."

And Abraham looked up and saw a ram caught in a thicket by its horns. And he went and took the ram and burned it as a sacrifice instead of his son. And he named that place YHVH-yireh, *The Lord Provides*.

And Abraham went back to his men, and they set out together for Beer-sheba. And Abraham stayed in Beer-sheba.

The Cave of Machpelah

P

And when Sarah was a hundred and twenty-seven years old, she died in Kiryat-arba (which is now Hebron), in Canaan. And Abraham made preparations to mourn for Sarah, and stood up from the ground where he had been sitting beside her body, and went and said to the Hittites, "I am an alien among your people, but please sell me a burial site, so that I can bury my dead."

And the Hittites answered Abraham, "Sir, you are a great lord among us. Bury your dead in the best grave we have; there is not one of us who will deny you his grave."

Then Abraham bowed low to the Hittites, the natives of the land. And he said to them, "If you wish to help me with the burial, persuade Ephron, son of Zohar, to sell me the cave of Machpelah, which is at the edge of his land. Let him sell it to me in your presence, at its full price, so that I can use it as a burial site."

And Ephron was there among the elders of the city. And he said to Abraham, "Sir, you may have that land, with its cave, as a gift from me; I give it to you in the presence of my people. Bury your dead there."

And Abraham bowed low to the elders and said to Ephron, "No, please: let me pay you for the land. Take the money for it, and let me bury my dead there."

And Ephron said, "Sir, a bit of land worth two hundred ounces of silver—what is a trifle like that between me and you? Go, bury your dead."

And Abraham nodded to Ephron, and he weighed out for him

the amount that he had named before the elders of the city: two hundred ounces of pure silver.

So Ephron's land in Machpelah, east of Mamre — the land, its cave, and all the trees within the boundaries of the land — became the property of Abraham in the presence of the elders of the Hittites. And after this Abraham buried his wife Sarah in the cave of Machpelah, east of Mamre (which is now Hebron), in Canaan.

The Betrothal of Rebecca

LATE SOURCE

Now Abraham was very old, and the Lord had blessed him in all things. And when the time of his death drew near, Abraham said to the slave who had been longest in his service and who was in charge of everything he owned, "Put your hand under my thigh and swear by the Lord, the God of heaven and earth, that you will not take a wife for my son Isaac from the Canaanite women here, but that you will go to my native land and my kinsmen and bring back a wife for him."

And the slave said, "What if the woman is not willing to come with me: should I take your son back to the land you came from?"

And Abraham said, "Don't take my son there for any reason. The Lord, who called me from my father's house and from the land where I was born and who promised me that he would give this land to my descendants — he will send his presence before you, and you will find a wife there for my son. And if the woman is not willing to come with you, then you are absolved from this oath. But you must never take my son back there." And the slave put his hand

<24:9>

under Abraham's thigh and swore that he would do as he had been commanded.

And he took ten camels from his master's herds and set out, with all his master's wealth at his disposal. And he traveled to Aram-naharayim, to the city of Nahor. And he made the camels kneel down by the well outside the city toward evening, when the women come out to draw water. And he prayed, "Lord, God of my master Abraham, please send me good luck today and keep faith with my master. Here I am, standing by the spring as the young women come out to draw water. I am going to say to one of them, 'Please pour me some water from your jar'; if she answers, 'Drink, and I will also give water to your camels,' let her be the one you have appointed for Isaac. That is how I will know you have kept faith with my master."

Before he had finished praying, Rebecca came out with her jar on her shoulder (she was the daughter of Nahor, Abraham's brother). And she was very beautiful, and of marriageable age, and had never slept with a man. And she went down to the spring and filled her jar. And as she came back, the slave ran to her and said, "Please give me a little water from your jar."

And she said, "Drink, sir," and quickly lowered her jar from her shoulder and gave him a drink. And when he had had enough, she said, "I will draw water for your camels too, until they have had enough." And she quickly emptied her jar into the trough and ran back to the well and drew water for all his camels. And the man stood gazing at her, wondering whether the Lord had made his errand successful.

And when the camels had finished drinking, he took out a gold

<2:24:22>

nose-ring weighing a quarter of an ounce and put it on her nose, and he put two bracelets weighing five ounces on her arms. And he said, "Tell me, please, whose daughter you are. And is there room for us in your father's house?"

And she said, "I am the daughter of Nahor. And yes, we have plenty of straw and fodder, and room for you to spend the night."

And the man bowed down to the Lord and said, "Blessed be the Lord, the God of my master Abraham, who has never stopped dealing kindly with my master. For he has led me straight to the house of my master's brother."

And Rebecca ran to her mother's house and told them what had happened.

And when Laban, her brother, saw the nose-ring and the bracelets on his sister's arms and heard her tell what the man had said, he ran out to the spring. And he found the man standing there beside the camels, and he said, "Welcome, sir, and come in; why are you standing out here when I have prepared the house and cleared a place for the camels?"

And he led the man to the house, and unloaded the camels, and gave them straw and fodder, and brought him and his men water to bathe their feet. But when food was set before him, the man said, "I will not eat until I have told my story."

And Laban said, "Tell it."

And he said, "I am Abraham's slave. And the Lord has blessed my master and made him very rich, and has given him sheep and oxen, silver and gold, male and female slaves, camels and donkeys. And Sarah, my master's wife, bore my master a son in her old age, and he has assigned him everything he owns. And my master made me

<24:37>

swear an oath, saying, 'You must not take a wife for my son from the Canaanite women here, but you must go to my father's house and my family, and bring back a wife for him.' And I said to my master, 'What if the woman is not willing to come with me?' And he said to me, 'The Lord, in whose ways I have walked, will send his presence with you and will bring you success, and you will find a wife for my son among my family and my father's house. Only if you come to my family and they refuse you, will you be absolved from this oath.' And today I came to the well and prayed, 'Lord, God of my master Abraham, please bring me success now. Here I am, standing by the spring, and I am going to say to one of the girls coming to draw water, "Please pour me some water from your jar"; if she answers, "Drink, and I will also draw water for your camels," let that be the woman the Lord has appointed for my master's son.' And before I had finished praying, Rebecca came out with her jar on her shoulder; and she went down to the spring and drew water. And I said to her, 'Please give me a drink.' And she quickly lowered her jar from her shoulder and said, 'Drink, and I will also give your camels water.' So I drank, and she also gave the camels water. And I asked her, 'Whose daughter are you?' And she said, 'The daughter of Nahor.' Then I put the ring on her nose and the bracelets on her arms, and I bowed down and blessed the Lord, the God of my master Abraham, who had led me on the right path to find the daughter of my master's brother for his son. And now tell me whether or not you intend to honor my master's wish, so that I can know what to do next."

Then Laban said, "This comes from the Lord; it is not for us to

<24:50>

approve or disapprove. Here is Rebecca: take her and go; let her be the wife of your master's son, as the Lord has decided."

And when Abraham's slave heard this, he bowed to the ground in thanksgiving to the Lord. Then he took out silver and gold jewelry and bridal garments, and gave them to Rebecca, and he gave costly presents to her brother and her mother. And he and his men ate and drank, and they spent the night there.

And in the morning he said, "Please give me permission to go back to my master."

And Rebecca's brother and mother said, "Let the girl stay with us for another week or so; then she can leave."

And he said, "Please don't keep me here, now that the Lord has brought me success. Give me permission to leave and return to my master."

And they said, "Let us call the girl and ask her." And they called Rebecca and said, "Are you willing to go with this man?"

And she said, "Yes."

So they sent Rebecca off, with her old nurse and Abraham's slave and his men. And they blessed her, saying, "Our sister, may you become multitudes, and may your descendants seize the gates of their enemies."

And Rebecca and her maids mounted the camels. And the slave took the reins of Rebecca's camel and left.

Now Isaac had moved on as far as Beer-lahai-ro'i and was living in the Negev. And one evening as he was out meditating in the fields, he looked up and saw the camels approaching.

And Rebecca looked up, and when she saw Isaac, she leaned

down from her camel and asked the slave, "Who is that man walking toward us?"

And the slave said, "That is my master." And she took her veil and covered herself.

And the slave told Isaac everything that had happened.

And Isaac brought Rebecca into his tent and took her as his wife. And he loved her, and was comforted after the death of his father.

The Death of Abraham; Ishmael's Descendants [P]

And Abraham assigned everything he owned to Isaac. And to his sons by the concubines he gave gifts while he was still alive, and he sent them to the east, for the benefit of his son Isaac.

And Abraham lived a hundred and seventy-five years, and he died at a ripe age, old and contented, and he was gathered to his ancestors. And his sons Isaac and Ishmael buried him in the cave of Machpelah, on the land of Ephron, son of Zohar the Hittite, east of Mamre, the land that Abraham had bought from the Hittites, where Abraham had buried his wife Sarah. And after the death of Abraham, God blessed his son Isaac; and Isaac settled near Beer-lahai-ro'i.

These are the descendants of Abraham's son Ishmael, whom Hagar the Egyptian, Sarah's slave, bore to Abraham. And Ishmael lived a hundred and thirty-seven years, and then he died and was gathered to his ancestors. And these are the names of the sons of Ishmael, in the order of their birth: Nebayoth, the firstborn, Kedar, Adbeel, Mibsam, Mishma, Dumah, Massa, Hadad, Tema, Jetur, Naphish, and Kedemah. These are the sons of Ishmael, by their settlements and their encampments: twelve chieftains of twelve tribes. And they lived between Havilah and Shur, which is east of Egypt, on the way to Asshur. And each lived at war with all his kinsmen.

Jacob and Esau

J

Now Rebecca was barren, and Isaac prayed to the Lord for her. And the Lord answered his prayer, and Rebecca conceived. And when it was time for her to give birth, twins came out of her womb. And the first one was red and hairy like a fur cloak; so they named him Esau, *The Shaggy One*. And then his brother came out, with one hand grasping Esau's heel; so they named him Jacob, *Heel-Grasper*.

And when the boys grew up, Esau became a skilled hunter, a man of the open country, and Jacob was a peaceful man who stayed near the tents. And Isaac loved Esau because he brought him venison to eat; but Rebecca loved Jacob.

One day, as Jacob was cooking a stew, Esau came back from hunting, and he was famished. And he said to Jacob, "Give me a heap of that red stuff: I'm famished."

And Jacob said, "First sell me your birthright."

And Esau said, "I am dying of hunger: what good is my birthright to me?"

And Jacob said, "Swear to me first." So he swore to him and sold him his birthright. Then Jacob gave Esau bread and lentil stew; and he ate and drank, and got up and went away. That is how Esau showed how little he valued his birthright.

Wife and Sister

VERSION 3: LATE SOURCE

Now there was a famine in the land — not the previous famine in the time of Abraham. And Isaac went to Gerar, to Abimelech, king of the Philistines. And the Lord appeared to Isaac and said, "Don't go down to Egypt; stay in this land, and I will be with you and bless you." So he stayed in Gerar.

And when the men of the city asked questions about Rebecca, he said that she was his sister, because he was afraid to say that she was his wife: he thought they would kill him and take her, because she was beautiful.

And after Isaac had been there for some time, Abimelech, king of the Philistines, looked down from his window one day and saw him making love to Rebecca. And Abimelech summoned him and said, "So she is your wife! How could you say she was your sister?"

And Isaac said to him, "I thought I would be killed because of her."

And Abimelech said, "What have you done to us! One of my people might have slept with your wife, and you would have brought punishment on us all." So Abimelech issued a command to his people: "Whoever touches this man or his wife will be put to death."

Isaac and Abimelech; Beer-sheba

VERSION 3: LATE SOURCE

And Isaac sowed seed in that land, and the same year he procured a hundred measures of barley, and the Lord blessed him. And he grew richer and richer, until he was very rich, with large flocks and herds and many slaves. And the Philistines were envious of him, and Abimelech said to him, "Leave us: you are much too strong for our comfort." And Isaac left and camped in the wadi of Gerar and settled there.

Now the Philistines had filled with dirt all the wells that his father Abraham's slaves had dug. And Isaac reopened the wells that the Philistines had stopped up after Abraham's death, and he called them by the names that his father had given them.

And when Isaac's slaves were digging in the wadi, they found a well of running water. But the shepherds of Gerar contested the claim of Isaac's shepherds and said, "This water belongs to us." So he named the well Esek, *Dispute*, because they had disputed with him. And when they dug another well, they contested that one too, so he named it Sitnah, *Accusation*. And he moved on from there and dug another well, and they didn't contest it, so he named it Rehovoth, *Room*, for he said, "The Lord has made room for us now, so that we can spread out in the land."

And from there he went up to Beer-sheba. And he pitched his tent there, and his slaves began digging a well.

And Abimelech came to him from Gerar, with his adviser Ahuzzath and Phicol, the commander of his army. And Isaac said,

<26:27>

"Why have you come here? You were hostile to me before, and drove me away."

And they said, "We see now that the Lord is with you, and we propose that the two of us swear an oath to each other and make a pact: you will not do us any harm, just as we have not harmed you but have always been kind to you and sent you away in peace. You are now entirely welcome here."

Then Isaac gave a feast for them, and they ate and drank. And in the morning they exchanged oaths, and Isaac sent them off, and they left in peace.

And that same day, Isaac's slaves came and told him about the well they had dug, and said to him, "We have found water." So he named it Shibah, *Oath*. That is why the city is called Beer-sheba, *The Well of the Oath*, to this day.

Esau Cheated of the Blessing
WHY JACOB WAS SENT TO LABAN, ACCORDING TO *J*

Now Isaac was old and his eyes had grown so dim that he couldn't see. And he called his elder son Esau and said to him, "My son."

And he said, "Yes."

And he said, "I am an old man now, and I may die any day. Take your quiver and bow, and go out to the open country and hunt me some venison. And cook me a stew, the way I like it, and bring it for me to eat, so that I can give you my blessing before I die."

Now Rebecca had been listening as Isaac spoke to his son Esau. And when Esau went out to hunt venison for his father, Rebecca

<27:6>

said to her son Jacob, "I just overheard your father telling your brother Esau to bring him some venison and cook him a stew so that he could eat and give him his blessing. Now listen and do exactly as I tell you. Go out to the flock and get me two tender kids, and I will cook them into a stew, the way your father likes it. Then you will take it in to your father, so that he can eat it and give you his blessing before he dies."

And Jacob said, "But Esau's skin is hairy, and mine is smooth. What if my father touches me and discovers the trick? I will bring a curse on myself, not a blessing."

And his mother said, "Let the curse be on me, my son. Just do as I say and get the kids."

So he went and got them and brought them to his mother, and she cooked a stew, the way his father liked it. And she took Esau's clothes and had Jacob put them on. And she covered his hands and the bare part of his neck with the goatskins. And she gave him the stew and the bread that she had baked.

And he went to his father and said, "Father."

And he said, "Yes? Who are you, my son?"

And Jacob said, "I am Esau, your firstborn. I have done as you told me to; sit up now and eat some of my venison, so that you can give me your blessing."

And Isaac said, "How did you get it so quickly, my son?"

And he said, "The Lord your God brought me good luck."

And Isaac said, "Come here and let me touch you, my son, to make sure that you are my son Esau."

And Jacob came close, and Isaac touched him and said, "The voice is Jacob's voice, but the hands are the hands of Esau." And

<27:23>

Isaac didn't recognize him, because his hands were hairy like Esau's hands. And he said, "Are you really my son Esau?"

And he said, "I am."

And he said, "Bring me the stew, my son, and I will eat and give you my blessing."

And he brought it to him, and he ate; and he brought him wine, and he drank. And Isaac said, "Come here and kiss me, my son." And he came close and kissed him. And Isaac smelled his clothes, and he blessed him and said,

> "How fragrant is my son's smell,
>> like the smell of the open country
>> that the Lord has blessed.
> May God give you the dew of heaven
>> and the richness of the dark earth:
>> an abundance of grain and wine.
> May you rule over your brother,
>> and may your mother's son bow before you.
> Cursed be those who curse you,
>> and may those who bless you be blessed."

No sooner had Jacob left his father Isaac than Esau came back from hunting. And he cooked a stew and brought it to his father and said, "Sit up, Father, and eat some of my venison, so that you can give me your blessing."

And Isaac said, "Who are you?"

And he said, "I am your son, your firstborn, Esau."

And Isaac shuddered violently and said, "Then who was it that brought me the other stew? I just finished eating it before you came, and I blessed him, and the blessing cannot be taken back."

<27:34>

And when Esau heard his father's words, he cried out loudly and bitterly and said, "Bless me, bless me too, Father."

And he said, "Your brother came and deceived me and took your blessing."

And he said, "Didn't you save a blessing for me?"

And Isaac said, "I gave him power over you, and made him your master, and granted him an abundance of grain and wine. What is left for you, my son?"

And Esau said, "Do you have just one blessing? Bless me too, Father." And he burst into tears.

And Isaac said,

> "Far from the richness of the dark earth
> > your home shall be,
> > far from the dew of heaven.
> By your sword you shall live,
> > and you shall be a servant to your brother."

And Esau hated Jacob because of the blessing that his father had given him, and he said to himself, "I will kill my brother Jacob, as soon as my father dies."

And when Rebecca guessed what her elder son Esau was thinking, she sent for her younger son Jacob and said to him, "Your brother Esau is planning to kill you in revenge. Listen to me now: you must leave right away and go to my brother Laban in Haran and stay with him for a while, until your brother's anger has died down and he has forgotten what you did to him. Then I will send for you and you can come back. Why should I lose you both in one day?"

<26:34>

Why Jacob Was Sent to Laban

ACCORDING TO P

Now when Esau was forty years old, he took as his wives Judith, daughter of Beeri the Hittite, and Basemath, daughter of Elon the Hittite. And this was a bitter grief for Isaac and Rebecca.

And Rebecca said to Isaac, "I am sick to death because of these Hittite women. If Jacob too takes a native woman as his wife, how can I go on living?"

So Isaac sent for Jacob and blessed him and said, "You must not take a Canaanite woman as your wife. Go right now to Paddan-aram, to the house of Bethuel, your mother's father; and take as your wife one of the daughters of Laban, your mother's brother. And may God Almighty bless you and make you fruitful and multiply you, so that you become a multitude of peoples. And may he give the blessing of Abraham to you and to your descendants, so that you may possess the land where you are now living, the land that God gave to Abraham."

Then Isaac sent Jacob off. And he went to Paddan-aram, to Laban, son of Bethuel the Aramean, brother of Rebecca, Jacob's and Esau's mother.

And when Esau learned that Isaac had given Jacob his blessing and commanded him not to take a Canaanite woman as his wife and sent him to Paddan-aram to find a wife there, and that Jacob had obeyed his father and mother and gone to Paddan-aram, Esau realized how greatly the Canaanite women displeased his father

<28:8>

Isaac. So he went to Ishmael and took Mahalath, daughter of Abraham's son Ishmael and sister of Nebayoth, as his wife, in addition to the wives that he already had.

Jacob at Beth-El

ACCORDING TO *J*

And Jacob set out from Beer-sheba and traveled toward Haran. And when he came to a certain place, he stopped for the night, because the sun had set.

And the Lord stood beside him and said, "I am the Lord, the God of your grandfather Abraham and the God of Isaac. I will be with you and will protect you everywhere you go, and I will bring you back to this land."

And Jacob woke up and said, "Truly, the Lord is present in this place and I didn't know it." And he named the place Beth-El, *The House of God.* (Before that, its name had been Luz.)

Jacob at Beth-El

ACCORDING TO *E*

And Jacob set out from Beer-sheba and traveled toward Haran. And when he came to a certain place, he stopped for the night, because the sun had set. And he took one of the stones of that place and put it near his head and lay down to sleep.

<28:12>

And he had a dream: he saw a staircase rising from the ground, and its top reached heaven, and God's angels were walking up and walking down it.

And he was filled with great awe and said, "How awesome this place is! This must be the house of God, and up there is the gateway to heaven."

And in the morning, Jacob took the stone that he had put near his head, and he set it up and poured oil on top of it. And he made a vow and said, "If God is with me and protects me on my travels and gives me food to eat and clothing to wear, and if I return safely to my father's house, then this stone that I have set up will be a house of God, and of everything you give me I will set aside a tenth for you." And he named the place Beth-El, *The House of God.*

Jacob and Rachel, and Leah
J

Then Jacob traveled on until he arrived in the east. And he looked around and saw a well in the open country, and three flocks of sheep were lying beside it. And the stone over the mouth of the well was very large: only when all the shepherds had gathered there could they roll the stone off the well and water the sheep and put the stone back.

And Jacob said to them, "Friends, where do you come from?"

And they said, "We are from Haran."

And he said, "Do you know Laban, son of Nahor?"

And they said, "Yes."

And he said, "Is he well?"

And they said, "Yes. And here comes his daughter Rachel with the sheep."

And he said, "It is still broad daylight, not yet time to gather the flocks. Why don't you water them and let them go on grazing?"

And they said, "We can't do that until all the shepherds are here to roll the stone off the well."

And while they were talking, Rachel came with her father's sheep (she was the one who took care of them). And when Jacob saw Rachel, he went up and rolled the stone off the well and watered Laban's sheep. And he kissed Rachel and burst into tears. And he told her that he was her father's kinsman — Rebecca's son. And she ran and told her father.

And when Laban heard that his sister's son Jacob had arrived, he ran to meet him, and he embraced him and kissed him again and again and took him home. And Jacob told Laban everything that had happened. And Laban said to him, "Truly, you are my flesh and blood."

And after Jacob had stayed with him for a month, Laban said, "Why should you serve me for nothing, just because you are my kinsman? Tell me what wages I should pay you."

Now Laban had two daughters: Rachel was the younger, and the elder was named Leah. And Leah had dull eyes, but Rachel was beautiful in face and body. And Jacob loved Rachel; and he said, "I will serve you seven years for Rachel, your younger daughter."

And Laban said, "All right. I would rather give her to you than to an outsider."

<29:20>

And Jacob served seven years for Rachel; and they seemed to him just a few days, so great was his love for her.

Then Jacob said to Laban, "My term is finished. Give me my wife now, so that I can sleep with her."

And Laban prepared a wedding feast, and all his neighbors came to celebrate. And in the evening, he got his daughter Leah and brought her to Jacob, and Jacob slept with her. And when morning came, he saw that it was Leah.

And he said to Laban, "How could you do this to me? Isn't Rachel the one I served you for? Why have you cheated me?"

And Laban said, "It is not our custom here to marry off the younger daughter before the firstborn. Wait a week, until the girl's wedding feast is over; then I will give you the other one too, if you will serve me for seven more years."

And Jacob agreed, and he waited until the week was over; then Laban gave him Rachel as his wife. And Jacob slept with Rachel too. And he loved Rachel more than Leah. And he served Laban for seven more years.

The Birth of Jacob's Children

J

And when the Lord saw that Leah was unloved, he opened her womb; but Rachel was barren. And Leah conceived and gave birth to a son, and she named him Reuben, *He Has Seen My Suffering*, for she said, "Surely the Lord has seen my suffering; now my husband will love me."

<30:1>

And when Rachel found that she was not bearing Jacob any children, she grew jealous of her sister; and she said to Jacob, "Give me children, or I will die."

And Jacob lost his patience with Rachel, and he said, "Do you think that I am God, who has denied you the fruit of the womb?"

And she said, "Here is my slave Bilhah: sleep with her, and I will adopt her children when she gives birth, so that through her I too may have children." And she gave him her maid Bilhah as a concubine. And Jacob slept with her, and Bilhah conceived and bore Jacob a son. And Rachel said, "God has vindicated me: he has heard my prayer and given me a son." So she named him Dan, *He Has Vindicated.*

One day, at the time of the wheat harvest, Reuben found some mandrakes in a field and brought them to his mother Leah. And Rachel said to Leah, "Please, give me some of your son's mandrakes."

And Leah said, "Isn't it enough that you have taken my husband? And now you want my son's mandrakes too!"

And Rachel said, "All right: give me the mandrakes and I will let him sleep with you tonight."

And when Jacob came home from the fields in the evening, Leah went out to meet him, and she said, "Tonight you are coming to my tent: I have hired you with my son's mandrakes." So he slept with her that night. And she conceived and bore Jacob a son. And Leah said, "God has given me my reward, because of what I gave my sister for my husband." So she named him Issachar, *He Has Rewarded.*

Then God remembered Rachel and opened her womb. And she conceived and gave birth to a son; and she said, "God has taken away my humiliation." So she named him Joseph, *He Has Taken Away.*

<30:25>

Jacob Outwits Laban

J

And after Rachel had given birth to Joseph, Jacob said to Laban, "With your permission, I would like to go back to my native land. You know how much my services have done for you. So give me my wives and children, whom I served you for, and let me go."

And Laban said, "If I have found favor with you, please stay. I have observed the omens and seen that the Lord has blessed me because of you. Decide on your own wages, and I will pay them."

And he said, "You know how well I have served you, and how your flocks have prospered under my care. They were small when I came, and now they have grown very large, and wherever I have gone the Lord has blessed you. But it is time that I provided for my own family."

And he said, "What do you want?"

And Jacob said, "Nothing of much value. Just do this for me, and I will take care of your animals as before: go through all your flocks today and take out every spotted and speckled animal, and these will be my wages. And whenever you come to check, it will be clear how honest I have been: if any of my animals are not speckled and spotted, you will know that they are stolen."

And Laban said, "All right, we will do as you say."

But that day Laban took out all the streaked and spotted animals and gave them to his sons to look after. And he put a three-day walk between himself and Jacob, while Jacob was tending the rest of Laban's flocks.

<30:37>

And Jacob took fresh poplar twigs and peeled off strips of bark from them. And he placed the peeled twigs upright in the watering troughs facing the animals. And the animals mated in front of the twigs, and they gave birth to speckled and spotted young. And whenever the stronger animals were mating, Jacob put the twigs in the troughs in front of them, so that they would mate facing the twigs. But when the weaker animals mated, he didn't put the twigs there. So the weaker animals went to Laban, and the stronger ones to Jacob.

And Jacob grew very rich, and he came to own large flocks, male and female slaves, camels, and donkeys.

Jacob's Flight

E?

Now Jacob noticed that Laban's conduct toward him was not as friendly as it used to be. And he heard that Laban's sons were saying, "Jacob has taken what rightfully belongs to our father, and all his wealth has been gotten at our father's expense."

So Jacob sent for Rachel and Leah, and they met him in the open country where he was tending his flocks. And he said to them, "I have noticed that your father isn't as friendly to me as he once was. You know that I have served your father faithfully, yet he has cheated me and changed my wages a dozen times. But God didn't let him do me any harm. When your father assigned me the speckled lambs and kids as my wages, nothing but speckled ones were born; when he assigned me the streaked lambs and kids as my wages, nothing

<31:8>

but streaked ones were born. Now last night God came to me in a dream and said, 'Jacob.' And I said, 'Yes.' And he said, 'I am the God who appeared to you at Beth-El, where you anointed the stone and made a vow to me. I have seen everything that Laban has done to you; go now, leave this land and return to the land where you were born.'"

And Rachel and Leah said to him, "We no longer have any share in our father's estate. Doesn't he treat us like outsiders, now that he has sold us and used up our purchase price? All the riches that God has taken from our father belong to us and our children. So do whatever God has told you to do."

Then Jacob put his children and his wives on camels, and he rode off with all his livestock. (Laban had gone away for the sheepshearing, and while he was gone, Rachel had stolen his idols.) So Jacob fled with everything he owned, and he crossed the Euphrates and headed toward the hill country of Gilead.

Three days later, Laban was told that Jacob had fled, and he took his kinsmen and pursued Jacob for seven days until he caught up with him in the hill country of Gilead. And he said to Jacob, "What have I done to make you carry off my daughters like captives in war? Why did you sneak away without saying a word about it to me? I would have seen you off with music and rejoicing, with tambourines and lyres. You didn't even give me a chance to kiss my daughters and grandchildren goodbye! That was a very stupid thing to do. I can understand that you had to leave because you were longing for your father's house; but why did you steal my gods?"

And Jacob said, "I didn't tell you because I was afraid you would force your daughters to stay. As for your gods, search my baggage: if

<31:32>

you find them with anyone here, that person dies." (Jacob didn't know that Rachel had stolen them.)

So Laban went into Jacob's tent and Leah's tent and the tents of the two maids, but he didn't find them. Then he went into Rachel's tent. Now Rachel had taken the idols and put them under her saddle cushion, and she was sitting on top of them. And she said to her father, "Please don't be angry, sir, if I don't stand up to greet you, but I have my period now." And Laban searched through the whole tent, but he didn't find the idols.

Then Jacob was angry, and he said to Laban, "What crime have I committed, to make you pursue me like this? You combed through all my possessions, but did you find a single thing that belongs to you? If you did, bring it here, show it to your kinsmen and mine, and let them decide between us. In the twenty years I was with you, did your ewes and she-goats ever miscarry? Did I ever slaughter your rams and eat them? When an animal was killed by wild beasts, didn't I make good the loss myself? Often the heat consumed me by day and the cold by night, and sleep fled from my eyes. Twenty years I served you: fourteen years for your two daughters, and six years for your flocks, though you changed my wages a dozen times. If the God of my father hadn't been with me, you would have sent me away empty-handed."

And Laban said, "These daughters are mine, these children are mine, these flocks are mine: everything you see is mine. Yet how can I harm my daughters or the children they have borne? Come now, let us make a pact, you and I: let us make a mound, and it will stand as a witness between us."

And Laban said to his kinsmen, "Gather stones." And they gath-

<31:46>

ered stones and made a mound. And Laban said, "This mound is a witness today between you and me: may God keep watch between us when we are out of each other's sight. If you ill-treat my daughters, or if you take other wives besides them — though no one else is there, God will be a witness between us."

And Jacob swore by the God of his father Isaac. Then Jacob offered a sacrifice on the hill, and invited his kinsmen to eat. And they ate and spent the night on the hill.

And in the morning Laban kissed his grandchildren and his daughters goodbye, and blessed them, and returned home.

Jacob Prepares to Meet Esau
J

And Jacob continued on his way, and angels of God met him. And when he saw them, he said, "This must be God's army"; so he named that place Mahanayim, *The Army.*

Then Jacob sent messengers ahead to his brother Esau in Seir. And he instructed them to give this message to Esau: "Sir, your brother Jacob humbly greets you and says, 'I have been staying with Laban and have been delayed until now, while I acquired oxen, donkeys, sheep, male and female slaves. And I am informing you of this, sir, in the hope that I may gain your favor.'"

And when the messengers returned to Jacob, they said, "We spoke to your brother Esau, and he is coming to meet you, and there are four hundred men with him."

<32:8>

And Jacob was very frightened. And he prayed, "God of my fathers, save me, I beg you, from my brother Esau; do not let him come and kill me, and the mothers and children too."

And he spent the night there, and in the morning he set aside a part of his herds as a gift for his brother Esau: two hundred she-goats and twenty he-goats, two hundred ewes and twenty rams, thirty milch camels with their calves, forty cows and ten young bulls, twenty she-donkeys and ten he-donkeys. And he put a slave in charge of each herd and said to them, "Go on ahead, and leave a space between the herds." And he said to the slave in front, "When my brother Esau meets you and asks who your master is and where you are going and who owns these animals you are herding, you say, 'Sir, they are Jacob's; he humbly sends them to you as a gift, sir, and he himself is coming behind us.'" And he gave the same instructions to the second and the third slave and to all the others who were driving the herds, telling each to say the same thing to Esau when they met him. (He was thinking, "First I will make atonement to him with the gift I have sent on ahead; then afterward, when I face him, perhaps he will forgive me.") So the gift went on ahead of him, while he spent the night in Mahanayim.

And during the night he got up and took his two wives, the two maids, and his eleven children, and crossed the ford of the Jabbok. And after he had taken them across the stream, he sent all his herds across.

<32:25>

Jacob Wrestles with God and Becomes Israel

ACCORDING TO J

And Jacob was left alone; and a being wrestled with him until dawn. And when the being saw that he couldn't defeat Jacob, he struck him on his hip socket, and Jacob's hip was wrenched out of joint.

And he said, "Let me go: dawn is coming."

And he said, "I will not let you go until you bless me."

And he said, "What is your name?"

And he said, "Jacob."

And he said, "Your name will no longer be Jacob, *Heel-Grasper*, but Israel, *He Who Has Struggled with God*, because you have struggled with God and you have won."

And Jacob said, "Please, tell me your name."

And he said, "You must not ask my name." And he left him there.

And Jacob named the place Penuel, *The Face of God*: "because I have seen God face to face, yet my life has been spared." And the sun rose on him as he passed through Penuel, and he was limping.

The Meeting of Jacob and Esau

J

And Jacob looked up and saw Esau coming, and there were four hundred men with him. And he divided the children among Leah,

Rachel, and the two maids, and he put the maids and their children in front, Leah and her children behind them, and Rachel and Joseph last. And he himself went on ahead, bowing to the ground seven times as he approached his brother. And Esau ran to meet him and threw his arms around him and kissed him and wept. And when he saw the women and the children, he said, "Who are these?"

And he said, "The children God has generously given me, sir."

Then the maids came forward with their children and bowed low. Next, Leah came forward with her children and bowed low. And last, Rachel and Joseph came forward and bowed low.

And Esau said, "And those herds — are they really a gift from you?"

And Jacob said, "I hope that you find my poor gift acceptable, sir."

And Esau said, "I have quite enough, my brother; keep what you have for yourself."

And Jacob said, "No, please, I beg you, as a sign of your favor, sir, please accept them as a gift from me. Seeing your face is like seeing the face of a god, you have received me so kindly. Please indulge me this once and accept the blessing I brought you: God has been generous to me, and I have much more than I need." And Jacob kept urging him until he accepted the gift.

Then Esau said, "Let us travel on together, and I will go alongside you."

And Jacob said, "Sir, you can see that the children are small, and the sheep and cattle are suckling their young; if they are driven hard for a single day, they will all die. Please, sir, go on ahead of me, and I will move along slowly, at the pace of the animals and children, and I will catch up with you in Seir."

<33:15>

And Esau said, "Let me at least leave some of my men with you as an escort."

And he said, "That is very kind of you, sir, but please don't bother."

So Esau started back to Seir. But Jacob went on to Succoth, and built a house for himself, and put up sheds for his cattle. That is why the place is called Succoth, *Sheds*.

Arrival in Canaan

P

And Jacob arrived safely at the city of Shechem, in Canaan, on his return from Paddan-aram; and he camped to the east of the city. And he bought the piece of land he had camped on from the sons of Hamor, Shechem's father, for a hundred pieces of silver. And he set up an altar there and called it El-Elohay-Yisrael, *God Is the God of Israel*.

The Rape of Dinah

EARLY SOURCE

Now Dinah, the daughter whom Leah had borne to Jacob, went out to visit some women of that region. And when Shechem, son of Hamor the Hivite, ruler of the region, saw her, he took her and slept with her by force. And he fell in love with Dinah, and he spoke

<34:3>

kindly to her and tried to win her heart. And he said to his father Hamor, "Get me this girl as my wife."

And Jacob heard that Shechem had violated his daughter Dinah. But since his sons were out with the livestock in the open country, Jacob did nothing until they returned. And when his sons heard what had happened, they came back, and they were outraged.

Then Hamor came out to Jacob to talk the matter over with him. And he said, "My son Shechem is in love with your daughter. Please give her to him as his wife."

And Jacob's sons answered, "We can't give our sister to a man who is uncircumcised — that is a disgrace among us."

And the young man lost no time in doing what they had said, because he greatly desired Jacob's daughter, and he had himself and his men circumcised. (He was the most respected man in his father's household.)

And on the third day, when the men were still in pain, two of Jacob's sons, Simeon and Levi, Dinah's full brothers, took their swords and entered the city unopposed. And they cut down Shechem and his men, and took Dinah from Shechem's house and left.

Then Jacob said to Simeon and Levi, "You have stirred up trouble for me and made me hateful to the people of this region. And since my numbers are few, they will join forces and attack me, and I will be destroyed, with all my family."

And they said, "Should we let our sister be treated like a whore?"

<35:1>

The Return to Beth-El

R

And God said to Jacob, "Go up now to Beth-El, and stay there and build an altar to the God who appeared to you when you were flee-ing from your brother Esau."

Then Jacob said to his household and to all the people who were with him, "Get rid of all your idols, purify yourselves, and put on fresh clothing. Then we will go up to Beth-El, and I will build an altar there to the God who answered me in my distress and who has been with me everywhere I have gone."

So they gave Jacob all their idols and the rings that were in their ears, and Jacob buried them under the terebinth tree near Shechem.

And Jacob and all the people who were with him came to Luz, in Canaan. And he built an altar there and named the place Beth-El, *The House of God*, because that was where God had revealed himself to him when he was fleeing from his brother.

And Deborah, Rebecca's old nurse, died and was buried under the oak tree below Beth-El, and Jacob called it Allon-bachuth, *The Oak of Tears.*

Jacob Becomes Israel

ACCORDING TO P

And when Jacob came from Paddan-aram, God appeared again to him and said, "I am God Almighty. Be fruitful and multiply; a

<35:11>

nation—a multitude of nations—will come from you, and kings will issue from your loins. And the land that I gave to Abraham and Isaac, I give to you and your descendants after you." And God blessed him and said, "Your name will no longer be Jacob, but Israel." Then God vanished from his sight.

And Jacob set up a stone on the place where he had spoken with him, and he poured an offering of wine and oil over it. And he named the place where God had spoken with him Beth-El, *The House of God.*

The Death of Rachel

J?

Then they set out from Beth-El; and when they were still some distance from Ephrath, Rachel went into labor, and she was in great pain. And when her pain was at its greatest, the midwife said to her, "Don't be afraid: you have another son." And as she breathed her last, she named the child Ben-oni, *Son of My Misfortune.* But his father called him Benjamin, *Son of the Right Hand.*

So Rachel died and was buried beside the road to Ephrath. And Jacob set up a stone over her grave, the same stone that is on Rachel's grave to this day.

<35:21>

Reuben Sleeps with Bilhah

J; FRAGMENTARY

And Israel traveled on and pitched his tent on the other side of Migdal-eder. And while Israel was staying in that region, Reuben slept with Bilhah, his father's concubine. And when Israel heard about it...

Jacob's Sons; The Death of Isaac [P]

The sons of Jacob were now twelve. The sons of Leah were Reuben, Jacob's firstborn, Simeon, Levi, Judah, Issachar, and Zebulun. And the sons of Rachel were Joseph and Benjamin. And the sons of Bilhah, Rachel's maid, were Dan and Naphtali. And the sons of Zilpah, Leah's maid, were Gad and Asher. These are the sons of Jacob who were born to him in Paddan-aram.

And Jacob went to his father Isaac at Mamre, in Kiryat-arba (which is now Hebron), where Abraham and Isaac had lived.

And when Isaac was a hundred and eighty years old, he died and was gathered to his ancestors, old and contented. And his sons Esau and Jacob buried him.

Genealogies [P]

These are the descendants of Esau. Esau took his wives from among the Canaanite women: Adah, daughter of Elon the Hittite, and Oholibamah, daughter of Anah, son of Zibeon the Horite, and Basemath, daughter of Ishmael and sister of Nebayoth. And Adah bore Esau Eliphaz, and Basemath bore Reuel, and Oholibamah bore Jeush, Jaalam, and Korah. These are the sons who were born to Esau in Canaan.

And Esau took his wives, his sons and daughters, and all the people of his household, his cattle and all his livestock, and all the possessions he had acquired in Canaan, and went to Seir, away from his brother Jacob. For their possessions were so great that they couldn't live together: the land where they were living couldn't support their livestock. So Esau lived in the hill country of Seir (Esau is Edom).

And these are the descendants of Esau, the ancestor of the Edomites, in the hill country of Seir. These are the names of Esau's sons: Eliphaz, son of Esau's wife Adah, and Reuel, son of Esau's wife Basemath. And the sons of Eliphaz were Teman, Omar, Zepho, Gatam, and Kenaz; Eliphaz also had a concubine named Timna, who bore him Amalek. These are the descendants of Esau's wife Adah. And these are the sons of Reuel: Nahath, Zerah, Shammah, and Mizzah; they were the descendants of Esau's wife Basemath. And these are the sons of Esau's wife Oholibamah, daughter of Anah, son of Zibeon: she bore Esau Jeush, Jaalam, and Korah.

These are the clans of the sons of Esau. The descendants of Esau's firstborn son Eliphaz: the clans of Teman, Omar, Zepho, Kenaz, Korah, Gatam, and Amalek. These are the clans of Eliphaz in Edom; they are the descendants of Adah. And these are the descendants of Esau's son Reuel: the clans of Nahath, Zerah, Shammah, and Mizzah. These are the clans of Reuel in Edom; they are the descendants of Esau's wife Basemath. And these are the descendants of Esau's wife Oholibamah: the clans of Jeush, Jaalam, and Korah. These are the clans of Esau's wife Oholibamah, daughter of Anah. These are the sons of Esau, and these are their clans.

These are the sons of Seir the Horite, the inhabitants of the land: Lotan, Shobal, Zibeon, Anah, Dishon, Ezer, and Dishan.

<36:21>

These are the clans of the Horites, the descendants of Seir in Edom. And the sons of Lotan were Hori and Hemam, and Lotan's sister was Timna. And these are the sons of Shobal: Alvan, Manahath, Ebal, Shepho, and Onam. And these are the sons of Zibeon: Ayah and Anah (this is the Anah who discovered the hot springs in the wilderness as he was tending his father's donkeys). And these are the children of Anah: Dishon and Anah's daughter Oholibamah. And these are the sons of Dishon: Hemdan, Eshban, Ithran, and Cheran. And these are the sons of Ezer: Bilhan, Zaavan, and Akan. And these are the sons of Dishan: Uz and Aran.

These are the clans of the Horites: the clans of Lotan, Shobal, Zibeon, Anah, Dishon, Ezer, and Dishan. These are the clans of the Horites, clan by clan, in Seir.

And these are the kings who reigned in Edom, before any king reigned over the Israelites. Bela, son of Beor, reigned in Edom, and the name of his capital was Dinhabah. And when Bela died, he was succeeded by Jobab, son of Zerah of Bozrah. And when Jobab died, he was succeeded by Husham, from the land of the Temanites. And when Husham died, he was succeeded by Hadad, son of Bedad, who defeated the Midianites in the territory of Moab, and the name of his capital was Avith. And when Hadad died, he was succeeded by Samlah of Masrekah. And when Samlah died, he was succeeded by Saul of Rehoboth-on-the-Euphrates. And when Saul died, he was succeeded by Baal-hanan, son of Akbor. And when Baal-hanan died, he was succeeded by Hadad, and the name of his capital was Pau, and his wife's name was Mehetabel, daughter of Matred, son of Mezahab.

And these are the names of the clans of Esau, according to their families and places, by their names: the clans of Timnah, Alvah, Jetheth, Oholibamah, Elah, Pinon, Kenaz, Teman, Mibzar, Magdiel, and Iram. These are the clans of Edom, according to their settlements in the land that they possessed.

<38:1>

Judah and Tamar

EARLY SOURCE

And Jacob settled in Canaan, where his father had lived.

At about that time Judah parted from his brothers and headed south, and he camped near a certain Adullamite named Hirah. And there he met the daughter of a Canaanite named Shua; and he took her as his wife and slept with her. And she conceived and gave birth to a son, and she named him Er. And she conceived again and gave birth to a son, and she named him Onan. And again she conceived and gave birth to a son, and she named him Shelah; she was at Chezib when she gave birth to him.

And Judah found a wife for Er, his firstborn, and her name was Tamar. But Er was wicked in the Lord's sight, and the Lord made him die. And Judah said to Onan, "Go and fulfill your obligation as a brother-in-law: sleep with your brother's widow, and produce a child for your brother." But Onan knew that the child would not count as his; so whenever he slept with his brother's widow, he spilled his seed, in order not to produce a child for his brother. And what he did was wicked in the Lord's sight, and he made him die too.

Then Judah said to Tamar, his daughter-in-law, "Go back to your father's house until my son Shelah grows up." (He was afraid that Shelah too would die, like his brothers.) So Tamar went back to her father's house.

Many years later, Judah's wife Bat-shua died. And after the period of mourning was over, Judah went up to Timnah for the sheepshearing, together with his friend Hirah the Adullamite. And someone said to Tamar, "Your father-in-law is coming to Timnah for the sheepshearing." Now Tamar knew that Shelah was grown up, yet she had not been given to him as a wife; so she took off her widow's clothes, wrapped herself up, covered her face with a veil, and sat down at the entrance gate to Enayim, which is on the road to Timnah.

And when Judah saw her, he thought that she was a prostitute, since her face was veiled. And he went over to her at the roadside and said, "Let me sleep with you," not realizing that she was his daughter-in-law.

And she said, "What will you pay me?"

And he said, "I will send you a kid from my flock."

And she said, "All right, but leave me a pledge until you send it."

And he said, "What kind of pledge?"

And she said, "Your seal and the staff you are holding."

So he gave them to her, and slept with her, and she became pregnant. Then she left and went home, and she took off her veil and put on her widow's clothes.

And Judah sent his friend the Adullamite with the kid, to get back the pledge from the woman; but he couldn't find her. And he asked the people of that place, "Where is the temple-prostitute, the one who was sitting by the roadside at Enayim?"

And they said, "There wasn't any temple-prostitute here."

So he returned to Judah and said, "I couldn't find her; furthermore, the people said there wasn't any temple-prostitute there."

And Judah said, "Let her keep the pledge; if I go on looking for her, I will make myself a laughingstock. I sent the kid, as I promised; I can't help it if you didn't find her."

About three months later Judah was told, "Your daughter-in-law Tamar is a whore, and she has gotten herself pregnant from her whoring."

And Judah said, "Bring her out to be burned."

And as she was being brought out, she sent a message to her father-in-law: "The man who got me pregnant is the owner of this seal and this staff; see if you recognize whose they are."

And Judah recognized them and said, "She is in the right and I am in the wrong, because I didn't give her to my son Shelah." But he never slept with her again.

And when it was time for her to give birth, it turned out that there were twins in her womb. And while she was giving birth, one of them put out a hand, and the midwife took it and tied a scarlet thread around the wrist and said, "This one came out first." But just then he pulled back his hand, and his brother came out. And she said, "What a breach you have made for yourself!" So she named him Perez, *Breach*. And then his brother came out, with the scarlet thread on his wrist; and she named him Zerah, *Bright One*.

Joseph and His Brothers

EARLY SOURCE

Now Jacob loved Joseph more than all his other sons, because he was a child of his old age, and he made him a coat of many colors.

And when Joseph's brothers saw that their father loved him more than all his other sons, they hated him, and they would not even greet him.

One night, Joseph had a dream, and in the morning he said to his brothers, "Listen to the dream I had! We were out in the field binding sheaves; and suddenly my sheaf stood up, and your sheaves formed a ring around mine and bowed down to it!"

And his brothers said, "So you are supposed to rule over us and be our king—is that what your dream means?" And they hated him even more.

Then he had another dream, and in the morning he said to his brothers, "Listen, I had another dream: the sun, the moon, and eleven stars were bowing down to me!"

And when his father heard about it, he scolded him and said, "What is the meaning of this dream of yours? Do you really think that I and your mother and your brothers will come and bow down before you?"

And his brothers were furious at him; but his father kept thinking about this for a long time afterward.

One day, when his brothers were tending the flocks near Shechem, Jacob said to Joseph, "Your brothers are at Shechem; will you go to them for me?"

And Joseph said, "Yes, Father."

And he said, "See how they and the flocks are doing, and bring me a report."

And Joseph traveled to Shechem. And his brothers saw him a long way off, and as he approached, they plotted to kill him. And

<37:19>

they said to one another, "Look, here comes the dreamer. Now is our chance: let's kill him and throw him into one of these pits and say that a wild beast ate him. Then we will see what good his dreams are."

And when Joseph reached his brothers, they stripped him of his coat and threw him into a pit. And the pit was empty; there was no water in it. Then they sat down to eat.

And when they looked up, they saw a caravan of Ishmaelites coming from Gilead on their way down to Egypt, their camels loaded with spices, balm, and myrrh. And Judah said to his brothers, "What will we gain by killing our brother and covering up his blood? Why not sell him to these Ishmaelites? Let us not harm him: after all, he is our own flesh." And his brothers agreed.

And they pulled Joseph up out of the pit and sold him for twenty pieces of silver to the Ishmaelites, who brought Joseph to Egypt.

Then they took Joseph's coat, and slaughtered a kid, and dipped the coat in its blood. And they brought it to their father and said, "We found this coat. See if it is your son's."

And he recognized it and said, "My son's coat! A wild beast ate him! Joseph is torn, torn!" Then Jacob ripped his clothes, and put sackcloth around his hips, and remained in mourning for his son for a very long time. And all his sons and daughters tried to comfort him; but he refused to be comforted, and he said, "I will go down to my son in the grave, mourning."

Now after Joseph had been taken down to Egypt, a certain Egyptian bought him from the Ishmaelites. And the Lord was with

Joseph, and he was successful in his master's household. And when his master saw that the Lord was with him and brought success to everything he did, he took a liking to Joseph. And he made him his personal attendant, and put him in charge of his whole household, and entrusted him with everything he owned. And from that moment, the Lord blessed his household for Joseph's sake, and the Lord's blessing was on everything he owned, in the house and in the fields. And he left everything in Joseph's hands, and he gave no thought to anything except the food he ate.

Now Joseph was beautiful in face and body. And after a while, his master's wife looked at him with desire, and she said, "Sleep with me."

But he refused and said, "Please, madam, my master has trusted me with everything in this house; he has held nothing back from me but you, since you are his wife. How can I do such a wicked thing, and sin against God?" And though she spoke to Joseph day after day, he would not consent to sleep with her.

One day, when he came in to do his work, none of the servants happened to be in that part of the house. And she grabbed him by his cloak and said, "Sleep with me!" But he got away, leaving his cloak in her hand, and ran out of the house.

And after he ran out, she shouted for the servants and said, "Look what happens when my husband brings in a Hebrew to fondle us! This fellow tried to rape me, but I screamed as loud as I could, and he ran out, leaving his cloak behind." And she kept the cloak beside her until his master came home.

And when he came home, she said to him, "The Hebrew slave

that you brought here tried to rape me, but I screamed, and he ran out, leaving his cloak behind."

And when his master heard his wife's story, he was enraged, and he had Joseph seized and thrown into prison. And there Joseph remained.

Some time later, Pharaoh got angry at two of his officials, the chief butler and the chief baker, and he put them under detention in the house of the captain of the guard — the same prison where Joseph was being held. And the captain of the guard assigned Joseph to them as their attendant. And they remained under detention for some time.

One morning, when Joseph came to them, he saw that they were disturbed. And he said to them, "Why do you look so upset today?"

And they said, "We both had dreams last night, but there is no expert here to interpret them."

And Joseph said, "True interpretations come from God. Why don't you tell me your dreams?"

And the chief butler said, "In my dream, I saw a vine in front of me. And there were three branches on the vine, and as soon as it budded, it blossomed, and its clusters ripened into grapes. And Pharaoh's cup was in my hand, and I picked the grapes and squeezed them into Pharaoh's cup and handed the cup to Pharaoh."

And Joseph said, "This is what your dream means. The three branches are three days. Within three days, Pharaoh will summon you and restore you to your position, and you will be handing Pharaoh his cup just as you did when you were his butler. But when all is well with you again, please do me this favor: speak of me to Pharaoh and help me get out of prison. I was kidnapped from the land of the Hebrews, and I have done nothing wrong here to make them put me in this dungeon."

And when the chief baker saw that the interpretation was favorable, he said to Joseph, "My dream was just like that: I saw three wicker baskets on my head. And in the top basket there were all kinds of baked goods for Pharaoh, and the birds were eating them from the basket on my head."

And Joseph said, "This is what your dream means. The three baskets are three days. Within three days, Pharaoh will summon you and hang you on a tree, and the birds will eat the flesh from your bones."

Now the third day was Pharaoh's birthday, and he gave a feast for all his officials, and he summoned the chief butler and the chief baker. And he restored the chief butler to his position, but he hanged the chief baker, just as Joseph had predicted.

But the chief butler gave no further thought to Joseph, and forgot him.

Two years later, Pharaoh had a dream: he was standing beside the Nile, and seven cows, beautiful and plump, came up out of the river and grazed in the reed grass. And close behind them seven other cows, ugly and gaunt, came up out of the river and stood beside them on the bank. And the gaunt, ugly cows ate the seven plump, beautiful ones. Then Pharaoh woke up.

And when he fell asleep again, he had a second dream: seven ears of grain, full and ripe, were growing on one stalk. And seven other

<41:6>

ears, thin and shriveled by the east wind, sprouted close behind them. And the thin ears swallowed the seven ripe, full ears. Then Pharaoh woke up; and it was a dream.

And in the morning his mind was troubled. And he summoned all the dream-interpreters and wise men of Egypt, and told them his dream, but none of their interpretations satisfied him. Then the chief butler spoke up and said to Pharaoh, "Forgive me for mentioning my offenses, but some time ago Pharaoh was angry at me and the chief baker, and he put us under detention in the house of the captain of the guard. And one night, each of us had a dream. And a young man was with us there, a Hebrew, a slave of the captain of the guard. And when we told him our dreams, he interpreted them for us. And everything turned out just as he predicted: I was restored to my position, and the baker was hanged."

Then Pharaoh summoned Joseph, and they ran out and brought him from the dungeon. And he shaved and changed his clothes and came in before Pharaoh. And Pharaoh said to Joseph, "I had a dream, but no one can tell me its meaning. I have heard about you; it is said that you know how to interpret dreams."

And Joseph said, "Not I but God will give Pharaoh the right answer."

And Pharaoh said, "In my dream, I was standing on the bank of the Nile, and seven cows, plump and beautiful, came up out of the river and grazed in the reed grass. And close behind them seven other cows, scrawny and very ugly and gaunt, came out; never have I seen such ugly cows in all Egypt. And the gaunt, ugly cows ate the first seven cows, the plump ones; and even after they had eaten them, no one could have told that they were in their bellies: they

<41:21>

were just as gaunt as before. Then I woke up. And in my second dream I saw seven ears of grain, full and ripe, growing on one stalk. And seven other ears, dry and thin and shriveled by the east wind, sprouted close behind them. And the thin ears swallowed the seven ripe ears. And I told all this to my dream-interpreters, but none of them could tell me the meaning."

And Joseph said, "Pharaoh's dream can have just one meaning. God has told Pharaoh what he is about to do: the seven healthy cows are seven years, and the seven healthy ears are seven years; the seven gaunt, ugly cows that came up behind them are also seven years, and so are the seven thin ears shriveled by the east wind — they are seven years of famine. That is what I meant when I said that God has shown Pharaoh what he is about to do. Seven years of great abundance are coming to Egypt; but after them there will be seven years of famine, and nothing will be left of all the abundance, and famine will consume the land. And not a trace of the abundance will be left in the land, so severe will the famine be. As for Pharaoh's having the dream twice: this means that God has decided on the matter and will soon bring it about. So now Pharaoh should look for a man who is farseeing and wise, and he should put him in charge of all Egypt. And Pharaoh should appoint supervisors over the land to gather all the surplus grain of these good years, to collect it under Pharaoh's authority and bring it into the cities and store it there. And that grain will be a reserve for the seven years of famine, and the land will not be destroyed."

And the plan pleased Pharaoh and all his officials. And Pharaoh said to his officials, "How could we find anyone equal to this man, who is filled with the spirit of God?" And Pharaoh said to Joseph,

"Since God has shown you all this, there is no one so farseeing and wise as you. Therefore I am putting you in charge of all Egypt, and all my people will obey your command; only in court matters will my authority be greater than yours." And Pharaoh took off his signet ring and put it on Joseph's finger, and dressed him in robes of fine linen, and hung a gold chain around his neck, and mounted him in the chariot of his second-in-command, and officers walked before him shouting, "Bow down! Bow down!"

Thus Pharaoh made Joseph ruler over all Egypt and said to him, "I am Pharaoh, and this is my command: without your approval no one will move a hand or a foot in all Egypt." And Pharaoh gave Joseph the name Zaphenath-paneah, *Through Him the Living God Speaks,* and he gave him as his wife Asenath, daughter of Potiphera, priest of On.

And when Joseph left Pharaoh, he traveled throughout Egypt. And during the seven abundant years, when the earth produced crops in profusion, he gathered all the surplus grain in Egypt and brought it into the cities—in each city he stored the grain of the fields around it. And Joseph collected vast quantities of grain, like the sands of the sea, until he could no longer measure it: it was beyond all measure.

And before the years of famine came, two sons were born to Joseph: he named the firstborn Manasseh, *He Who Causes to Forget,* meaning, "God has made me forget all my hardship and my exile"; and he named the second son Ephraim, *Fruitful,* meaning, "God has made me fruitful in the land of my misfortune."

Then the seven years of abundance came to an end, and the seven years of famine began, just as Joseph had predicted. And when the

< 41:55 >

famine spread through all the land of Egypt, the people cried out to
Pharaoh for food. And Pharaoh said to them, "Go to Joseph; do
whatever he tells you." And Joseph opened all the storehouses and
sold grain to the Egyptians. And the famine grew more severe in
Egypt, and it spread over all the earth. And people from every country came to Joseph in Egypt to buy grain, so severe was the famine
over all the earth.

When Jacob learned that there was grain in Egypt, he said to his
sons, "Go down to Egypt and buy grain for us, so that we can stay
alive and not starve to death." So ten of Joseph's brothers went down
to buy grain in Egypt; only Benjamin, Joseph's full brother, had to
stay home, because Jacob was afraid that he would meet with some
disaster.

Now Joseph was the one who sold grain to all the people. And
Joseph's brothers came to him, and they bowed to the ground before
him. And when Joseph saw his brothers, he recognized them, but
he didn't let them know it. And he spoke harshly to them and said,
"Where have you come from?"

And they said, "From Canaan, to buy food."

And Joseph remembered the dreams he had had about them.
And he said to them, "You are spies; you have come to search out the
weak points in our defenses."

And they said, "No, my lord, we have come to buy food. We are
all sons of the same father. We are honest men; we are not spies."

And he said, "No: you have come to search out our weaknesses."

And they said, "We are twelve brothers, my lord, sons of one man back in Canaan. But the youngest is at home with our father, and one of us is gone."

And Joseph said to them, "As to what I said — that you are spies — this is how you will be tested: I swear by Pharaoh that you will not leave this place unless your youngest brother comes here. Choose one among you to go and get your brother; the rest will remain in prison until your story is verified. Otherwise, by Pharaoh, you are spies." And Joseph put them under detention for three days.

And on the third day, he said to them, "Do what I say and your lives will be spared, since I am a God-fearing man. If you are really honest men, one of you will remain in prison as a hostage, while the rest go and take home grain for your starving families. But you must bring me your youngest brother, to prove that you are telling the truth, and I will let you live."

And they said to one another, "We are being punished for what we did to our brother, because we saw his anguish when he pleaded with us, but we wouldn't listen. That is why this anguish has over-taken us."

And they didn't realize that Joseph understood their words (he was speaking to them through a translator). And he turned away from them and wept. And when he was able to face them again, he took Simeon and had him put in chains before their eyes; then he sent them away. And he gave orders to fill their baggage with grain, to put back each one's purchase money into his bag, and to give them provisions for their trip; and all this was done. And they loaded the grain onto their donkeys and left.

And when they stopped for the night, one of them opened his

bag to get fodder for the donkey, and there, at the top of the pack, was his money. And he said to his brothers, "My money has been returned! Here it is, in my pack!"

And their hearts stopped, and trembling they looked at one another and said, "What has God done to us?"

And when they came to their father Jacob in Canaan, they told him everything that had happened to them and said, "The man who is lord of the country spoke harshly to us and accused us of being spies. And we said to him, 'We are honest men; we are not spies. We are twelve brothers, sons of the same father, but one of us is gone, and the youngest is with our father in Canaan.' Then the man who is lord of the country said to us, 'This is how I will know if you are honest men: leave one of your brothers with me and take home grain for your starving families. But bring me your youngest brother, and then I will know that you are honest men and not spies, and I will return your brother to you, and you will be free to go wherever you want.'"

And Jacob said to them, "You are bereaving me of my children: Joseph is gone, Simeon is gone, and now you want to take Benjamin. It is more than I can bear. I will not let my son go down with you: his brother is dead, and he alone is left. And if he met with some disaster along the way, you would send my white head down to the grave in sorrow."

But the famine was still severe. And when they had used up all the grain they had brought from Egypt, their father said to them, "Go back and buy us some more grain."

<43:3>

And Judah said, "The man warned us not to appear before him unless our brother was with us. If you let our brother go with us, we will go down and buy your food. But if you won't let him, we can't go, since the man told us not to appear before him unless our brother was with us."

And Jacob said, "Why did you tell the man you had another brother, and cause me such grief?"

And they said, "The man questioned us about our family:'Is your father still alive? Do you have another brother?' We had to answer his questions. How could we know that he would order us to bring our brother?"

And Judah said to his father, "Send the boy in my care, and let us get started, so that we can stay alive and not starve to death — you, we, and our children. I take full responsibility for him; if I don't bring him back to you, let me bear the blame forever. If we hadn't wasted all this time, we could have been there and back by now."

And Jacob said to them, "If you must take him, do this: put our best products in your baggage and bring them to the man as gifts: some balm, some honey, spices and myrrh, pistachios and almonds. And take double the amount of money so that you can return the money you found in your packs; perhaps it was a mistake. Now take your brother, and go back to the man. And may God Almighty move the man to be compassionate to you and to let your other brother go, and Benjamin as well. But I — I am bereaved, bereaved."

So they took the gifts, and double the amount of money, and Benjamin, and they set out. And they went down to Egypt and presented themselves before Joseph. And when Joseph saw Benjamin with them, he said to his steward, "Bring these men home, and have an animal slaughtered and prepare a meal: these men will eat with me at noon."

And the steward brought the men to Joseph's house, as he had been ordered. And they were frightened as they approached it; they thought, "It must be because of the money in our packs that we are being brought here; he wants to seize us and our donkeys and make us slaves." So they went up to Joseph's steward at the entrance of the house and said to him, "We beg your pardon, sir, but we came down here once before to buy food. And on our way back, when we stopped for the night and opened our packs, each of us found his money, in full, at the top of his pack. So we have brought it back with us. And we also brought more money to buy food. We don't know who put the money in our packs."

And he said, "Don't be afraid; everything is all right; I did get your money. It must have been your God, the God of your father, who hid the treasure in your packs."

Then he brought Simeon out to them. And he brought them into Joseph's house, and gave them water to wash their feet and fodder for their donkeys. And they laid out their gifts for Joseph's arrival at noon, since they were told that they would be eating with him.

And when Joseph came home, they presented him with the gifts and bowed to the ground before him. And he greeted them and said, "How is your aged father? Is he still alive?"

And they answered, "Our father is alive and well, my lord." And they bowed low.

And Joseph looked at his brother Benjamin, his own mother's

<43:29>

son, and said, "This must be your youngest brother, whom you said you would bring to me." And he said, "May God be gracious to you, my son." And he hurried out: his heart was overwhelmed with love for his brother, and he could no longer hold back his tears. And he went to his room and wept.

Then he washed his face, and composed himself, and came out and said, "Serve the meal." And they served him separately, and his brothers separately, and the Egyptians who were eating with him separately (Egyptians are not permitted to eat with Hebrews; that is considered unclean). And he seated them in order of their ages, the eldest first and the youngest last; and they looked at one another in amazement. And he sent them each a portion from his table, but Benjamin's portion was five times larger than the others. And they feasted and got drunk with him.

Then Joseph said to his steward, "Fill the men's packs with as much grain as they will hold, and put my silver cup in the pack of the youngest." And he did what Joseph had told him.

Daylight came, and the men were sent off with their donkeys. And when they had gone just a short distance from the city, Joseph said to his steward, "Go, follow those men, and when you catch up with them, say, 'Why have you repaid good with evil and stolen my master's silver cup — the one he drinks from and looks into to see what lies hidden? That was a shameful thing to do!'"

And when he caught up with them, he repeated Joseph's words. And they said, "How can you accuse us of such a thing, sir? Heaven forbid that we do a thing like that! Look, the money we found in our packs: didn't we bring it back to you all the way from Canaan?

<44:8>

Then how could we steal silver or gold from your master's house? If it is found with any of us, sir, put that man to death and make the rest of us slaves."

And he said, "What you propose is fair; nevertheless, if it is found with any of you, only that man will be a slave; the rest will go free."

Then each of them quickly took down his pack and opened it. And the steward searched them, beginning with the eldest and ending with the youngest. And the cup was found in Benjamin's pack.

Then they ripped their clothes, and each man reloaded his donkey, and they went back to the city. And when Judah and his brothers entered Joseph's house, they prostrated themselves before him. And Joseph said to them, "How could you do a thing like this? Didn't you know that a man like me sees what lies hidden?"

And Judah said, "What can we say to you, my lord? How can we claim that we are innocent? God has uncovered our crime. We come here as your slaves, my lord, the rest of us as well as the one who was found with the cup."

And he said, "Heaven forbid that I do a thing like that! Only the one who was found with the cup will be my slave. The rest of you may go back to your father in peace."

Then Judah approached him and said, "I beg your indulgence, my lord: let me speak a word or two, please; don't lose patience with me; listen to what I say, even though you are as great as Pharaoh. You asked us, my lord, if we had a father or a brother. And we told you that we had an aged father and a child of his old age, a young boy, whose full brother is dead, so that he alone is left of his mother's children, and his father loves him. And you said to us, 'Bring him down to me, and I will look after him.' And we said to you, my lord, 'The boy cannot leave his father; if he left, his father would die.' But you said to us, 'Unless your youngest brother comes down with you, you will not be admitted into my presence.' And when we went back to our father, we told him what you had said, my lord. Later on, our father said, 'Go back and buy us some grain.' And we said, 'We can't go back. Only if our youngest brother is with us can we go; we will not be admitted into the man's presence unless our youngest brother is with us.' And our father said to us, 'You know that my wife bore me two sons. One son was taken from me, and I said, "He has been torn to pieces!" and I have never seen him again. And now you want to take this one too, and if he met with some disaster you would send my white head down to the grave in anguish.' And so, my lord, if I go back to our father and the boy is not with us — since his life is so bound up with his — when he sees that the boy is not with us, he will die of grief, and it will be our fault. I told my father that I would take full responsibility for the boy and that if I didn't bring him back, I would bear the blame forever. And so I beg you, my lord, please, let me stay here as your slave instead of the boy, and let him go up with his brothers. Because if the boy is not with me, how can I go back to my father, how can I look at the suffering that will overtake him?"

And Joseph could no longer control himself in front of all his attendants, and he shouted, "Everyone leave my presence!" So no one else was there when he made himself known to his brothers. But his sobbing was so loud that all the Egyptians could hear it.

Then Joseph said to his brothers, "I am Joseph. Is my father really alive?"

<45:3>

And his brothers couldn't answer, so terrified were they as they faced him.

Then Joseph said, "Come closer to me." And when they came closer, he said, "I am your brother Joseph, whom you sold into Egypt. Don't be troubled now, and don't blame yourselves for selling me, because God sent me ahead of you to save lives. For two years now the famine has gripped the land, and there will be five more years without a harvest. But God sent me ahead of you, and he has made me a father to Pharaoh, and master of all his household, and ruler over all Egypt. So it was not you but God who sent me here. Hurry back to my father and tell him that his son Joseph sends him this message: 'God has made me ruler over all Egypt. Come down to me right away; you will live in the region of Goshen, and you will be near me — you, your children and grandchildren, your flocks and herds, and everything you own. And I will take care of you there, and I will make sure that you and your household have everything you need, because there are five more years of famine ahead.' You can see for yourselves, and my brother Benjamin can see, that I really am Joseph. Tell my father about all the splendor that is mine in Egypt, and tell him about everything you have seen; and bring my father down here as quickly as you can."

And he threw his arms around his brother Benjamin and wept, and Benjamin wept too. And he kissed all his brothers and wept as he embraced them. And only then were his brothers able to speak to him.

And when the news reached Pharaoh's palace that Joseph's brothers had come, Pharaoh and his officials were pleased. And

<45:17>

Pharaoh said to Joseph, "Tell your brothers, 'This is what you must do: load your animals, take wagons out of Egypt for your children and wives, and go to Canaan. And get your father and your families and come back to me. And I will give you the best of Egypt, and you will eat the finest produce of the land. And don't worry if you have to leave some of your belongings behind: the best of Egypt is yours.'"

And Joseph gave them wagons, as Pharaoh had commanded, and supplies for the trip. To each of them he gave an ornamented robe, but to Benjamin he gave three hundred pieces of silver and five ornamented robes. And to his father he sent ten donkeys loaded with the best produce of Egypt, and ten she-donkeys loaded with grain, bread, and food for his trip. And he sent his brothers off.

And they went up from Egypt and came to their father Jacob in Canaan. And they said to him, "Joseph is still alive! He is ruler over all Egypt!" And his heart went numb: he couldn't believe them. But when they told him everything that Joseph had said, and when he saw the wagons that Joseph had sent to bring him back, his spirit revived. And Jacob said, "It is enough: my son Joseph is still alive. I will go and see him before I die."

And the sons of Israel took their father Jacob and their children and their wives in the wagons that Pharaoh had sent them, and they went to Goshen. And Jacob sent Judah ahead to Joseph; and Joseph ordered his chariot and went up to Goshen to meet his father. And when Joseph saw him, he threw his arms around him, and they wept and embraced for a long time. And Jacob said to Joseph, "Now I can die, since I have seen that you are still alive."

Then Joseph said to his brothers, "I will go up and tell the news to

Pharaoh and say, 'My brothers and my father's household have come to me from Canaan. They are shepherds, and they have brought their flocks and herds and everything they own.' And when Pharaoh summons you and asks what your occupation is, you must answer, 'We have been cattle-breeders all our lives, your majesty, as our ancestors were before us.' That is what you must say if you are to settle in Goshen, because the Egyptians think that all shepherds are unclean."

Then Joseph went to Pharaoh and said, "My father and my brothers have come from Canaan with their flocks and herds and everything they own, and they are now in Goshen." And he presented five of his brothers to Pharaoh.

And Pharaoh said to them, "What is your occupation?"

And they said, "We are shepherds, your majesty, as our ancestors were before us, and we have come to stay for a while in this region, since there is no land in Canaan where we can pasture our flocks, the famine is so severe there. So we beg you, your majesty, to let us live in Goshen."

And Pharaoh said to Joseph, "Now that your father and your brothers have come to you, all Egypt is open for them to live in; have them settle in Goshen, in the best part of the region. And if you know of any capable men among them, make them officers in charge of the royal herds."

So Joseph settled his father and brothers in the best part of the region, as Pharaoh had commanded. And Joseph provided food for his father and brothers and for all his father's household, down to the youngest child.

<47:27>

So Jacob settled in Egypt, in the region of Goshen.

And when the time of his death drew near, he called Joseph to his bedside and said, "Please put your hand under my thigh and promise that you will carry out my last wish: don't bury me in Egypt. When I lie down with my ancestors, take me out of Egypt and bury me in my grave."

And he said, "I will do whatever you wish."

And he said, "Swear it to me." So he swore it. And Jacob bowed his head as he lay there.

Some time later, Joseph was told, "Your father is failing." So he took his two sons, Manasseh and Ephraim, and went to Jacob. And when Jacob heard that Joseph had come, he summoned all his strength and sat up in bed.

And Jacob saw Joseph's sons, and he said, "Who are these?"

And Joseph said, "They are my sons, whom God has given me here."

And he said, "Bring them to me, and I will bless them." So Joseph brought them close to him, and Jacob kissed them and embraced them.

And he said to Joseph, "I thought I would never see you again, and now God has let me see your children too."

Then Joseph took them from his father's knees and bowed low to him.

And Jacob sent for all his sons, and he blessed them, with a special blessing for each. Then he drew his feet up onto the bed and died.

And Joseph bent down over his father's face and wept on him and kissed him. Then he ordered the physicians in his service to embalm his father, and it took them forty days. And there was mourning throughout Egypt for seventy days. And when the mourning period was over, Joseph said to Pharaoh's high officials, "Please do me this favor: speak to Pharaoh on my behalf, and tell him that on his deathbed my father made me swear that I would bury him in the grave he had bought for himself in Canaan. So would Pharaoh please be so gracious as to let me go up to Canaan and bury my father?"

And Pharaoh sent word: "Go up and bury your father, as you swore to do."

So Joseph went up to Canaan to bury his father, and with him went all the senior officials of Pharaoh's court, and all the dignitaries of Egypt, and all Joseph's household, and his brothers, and his father's household. Only their children and their flocks and herds stayed behind in Goshen. And many chariots and horsemen went with him; it was a very grand procession. And when they came to Goren ha-Atad, on the other side of the river, they held a very grand and solemn ceremony.

Then Joseph returned to Egypt with his brothers and all those who had gone with him to bury his father.

APPENDIXES

Appendix 1: Addenda to the Joseph Story

JACOB'S VISION AT BEER-SHEBA (LATE SOURCE) [46:1-5a]

And Israel set out with everything he owned. And when he reached Beer-sheba, he offered sacrifices to the God of his father Isaac.

And God spoke to Israel in a vision by night and said, "Jacob, Jacob." And he said, "Yes."

And he said, "I am God, the God of your father. Don't be afraid to go down to Egypt: I will make you into a great nation there. I will go down to Egypt with you, and I myself will bring you back up. And when you die, Joseph will close your eyes."

Then Jacob set out from Beer-sheba.

THE DEPARTURE FOR EGYPT (P) [46:6-7]

And they took their livestock and the possessions they had acquired in Canaan and came to Egypt—Jacob and all his offspring. He brought his sons and his grandsons, his daughters and his granddaughters—all his offspring—with him into Egypt.

GENEALOGIES (P) [46:8-27]

These are the names of the Israelites, Jacob and his descendants, who came to Egypt: Reuben, Jacob's firstborn; and Reuben's sons: Enoch, Pallu, Hezron, and Carmi. And Simeon's sons: Jemuel, Jamin, Ohad, Jachin, Zohar, and Saul, the son of a Canaanite woman. And Levi's sons: Gershon, Kohath, and Merari. And Judah's sons: Er, Onan, Shelah, Perez, and Zerah (but Er and Onan had died in Canaan); and Perez's sons were Hezron and Hamul. And Issachar's sons: Tola, Puvah, Jashub, and Shimron. And Zebulun's sons: Sered, Elon, and Jahleel. These were

Leah's descendants, whom she bore to Jacob in Paddan-aram, in addition to his daughter Dinah. These sons and daughters numbered thirty-three in all.

And Gad's sons: Ziphion, Haggi, Shuni, Ezbon, Eri, Arodi, and Areli. And Asher's sons: Imnah, Ishvah, Ishvi, and Beriah, with their sister Serah; and Beriah's sons were Heber and Malchiel. These were the descendants of Zilpah, whom Laban gave to his daughter Leah, and she bore these to Jacob: sixteen people.

The sons of Jacob's wife Rachel: Joseph and Benjamin. And Manasseh and Ephraim were born to Joseph in Egypt, by Asenath, daughter of Potiphera, priest of On. And Benjamin's sons: Belah, Becher, Ashbel, Gera, Naaman, Ahiram, Shupham, Hupham, and Ard. These were Rachel's descendants, whom she bore to Jacob. They numbered fourteen in all.

And Dan's son: Hushim. And Naphtali's sons: Jahzeel, Guni, Jezer, and Shillem. These were the descendants of Bilhah, whom Laban gave to his daughter Rachel, and she bore these to Jacob. They numbered seven in all.

The people who went to Egypt with Jacob — his bodily descendants, not including the wives of his sons — numbered sixty-six in all. And the sons of Joseph, who were born to him in Egypt, numbered two. The people in Jacob's family who went to Egypt numbered seventy in all.

JACOB IN EGYPT (P) [47:7-11, 27b-28]

Then Joseph brought in his father and introduced him to Pharaoh, and Jacob greeted Pharaoh. And Pharaoh said to Jacob, "How old are you?"

And Jacob said to Pharaoh, "I have lived for a hundred and thirty years. Few and bitter have my years been, far fewer than the years that my ancestors lived." Then Jacob took leave of Pharaoh and departed.

And Joseph settled his father and brothers, and he gave them property in Egypt, in the land of Rameses. And they acquired property there, and they were fruitful and multiplied greatly. And Jacob lived in Egypt for seventeen years, so that the years of his life were a hundred and forty-seven.

JOSEPH'S LAND POLICY (LATE SOURCE) [47:13-26]

Now there was no food anywhere in the country, so severe was the famine, and Egypt and Canaan languished. And Joseph collected all the money in Egypt and in Canaan as payment for the grain, and he put it into Pharaoh's treasury.

And when there was no more money in Egypt and in Canaan, all the Egyptians came to Joseph and said, "All our money is gone. Give us food or we will die before your eyes."

And Joseph said, "If your money is gone, give me your livestock, and I will give you food." So they brought their livestock to Joseph, and Joseph gave them food in exchange for their horses, sheep, oxen, and donkeys. Thus he supplied them with food in exchange for all their livestock that year.

When that year was over, they came to him again and said, "My lord, we cannot hide it from you that since our money is gone and our livestock belongs to you, we have nothing left to offer you, my lord, but our bodies and our land. Why should we die before your eyes, we and our land as well? Take us and our land in payment for food, and we and our land will be slaves to Pharaoh. (variant:) *And give us seeds so that we can stay alive, or we will starve to death and the land will turn into a desert.*"

So Joseph bought up all the land in Egypt for Pharaoh; all the Egyptians sold their fields, because the famine was too harsh for them, and the land became Pharaoh's. And Joseph made the people slaves from one end of Egypt to the other. The only land he didn't buy was the priests' land: they had a fixed income from Pharaoh, and they lived off this income, so they didn't have to sell their land.

(variant:) Then Joseph said to the people, "Now that I have bought you and your land for Pharaoh, here is seed for you to sow the land. Every time there is a harvest, you must give a fifth of it to Pharaoh, but four-fifths will be yours, to sow the fields and to feed yourselves and your families."

And they said, "You have saved our lives. We thank you, my lord, and we will be Pharaoh's slaves." And Joseph made it a law over Egypt (it is in effect to this day) that a fifth of all the land's produce must be given to Pharaoh.

JACOB ADOPTS JOSEPH'S SONS (P) [48:3-7]

And Jacob said to Joseph, "God Almighty appeared to me at Luz, in Canaan, and blessed me and said to me, 'I will make you fruitful and multiply you, so that you will become a multitude of peoples; and I will give this land to your descendants as an everlasting possession.' And now your two sons, who were born to you in Egypt before I came here, will be counted as my sons; Ephraim and Manasseh will be mine, as Reuben and Simeon are. But the children born to you after them will be counted as yours, and in matters of tribal territory they will be counted under their elder brothers' names." *(later addition:) "And when I returned from Paddan, Rachel died beside me in Canaan, along the way, when we were still some distance from Ephrath, and I buried her there beside the road to Ephrath, which is now Bethlehem."*

JACOB BLESSES JOSEPH'S SONS (A LATER VERSION: LATE SOURCE)
[48:13, 10a, 14-22]

And Joseph took them both and brought them close to Israel—Ephraim on his right, to Israel's left, and Manasseh on his left, to Israel's right. (Israel's eyes had grown weak with age; he couldn't see.) But Israel, crossing his hands, stretched out his right hand and put it on Ephraim's head, though he was the younger, and put his left hand on Manasseh's head, though he was the firstborn.

(later addition:) And he blessed Joseph and said, "May the God on whose paths

my fathers Abraham and Isaac walked, the God who has been my shepherd all my life, to this day, the presence who has rescued me from all harm, bless the boys; may my name live on in them, and the names of my fathers Abraham and Isaac; and may they grow into multitudes on the earth."

And when Joseph saw that his father had put his right hand on Ephraim's head, he was displeased, and he took hold of his father's hand, to move it from Ephraim's head to Manasseh's; and he said, "Not like that, Father. *This* one is the firstborn; put your right hand on *his* head."

But his father refused and said, "I know, my son, I know. He too will become a tribe, and he too will be great. But his younger brother will be even greater, and his descendants will become a multitude of nations." *(later addition:) And he blessed them that day and said, "By you will Israel bless itself and say: 'May God make you like Ephraim and like Manasseh.'"* Thus he gave Ephraim precedence over Manasseh. *(appendage 1:) Then Israel said to Joseph, "I am about to die. But God will be with you and will bring you back to the land of your fathers." (appendage 2:) "And now I give you—over and above your brothers' portion—one ridge [or: Shechem], which I captured from the Amorites with my sword and bow."*

THE TESTAMENT OF JACOB (EARLY SOURCE) [49:1b-28bα]
(editorial addition:) And Jacob said, "Gather around, and I will tell you what will happen to you in the time to come:

> *Assemble and listen, you sons of Jacob;*
> *hear the words of Israel your father.*

You, Reuben, are my firstborn son,
    the first fruit of my manhood's vigor,
    foremost in rank, foremost in strength.
Impetuous as water, you shall no longer be first;
    for you climbed up and took your father's wife:
    shamelessly you polluted my bed.

Simeon and Levi: two of a kind;
      tools of violence are their swords.
For in their fury they killed a man,
      and in their vengeance they slaughtered a prince.
Cursed be their fury and their savage pride;
      cursed be their wrath and their ruthlessness.
Therefore I will disperse them in Jacob,
      and throughout all Israel they shall be scattered.

You are Judah, praised by your brothers;
      the sons of your father bow before you;
      your strong hand seizes your enemies' necks.
Fierce as a lion's cub is Judah;
      he climbs from the valley after killing his prey.
He crouches like a lion inside his den;
      as he lies there, who would dare to arouse him?
The scepter shall not depart from Judah,
      nor the staff of power from between his feet,
until his anointed ruler comes,
      to whom all Canaan shall bend its knee.
He ties his donkey to a grape-heavy vine
      and tethers it by the deep-purple fruit.
He washes his clothes in vats of wine;
      he soaks his garments in the blood of grapes.
Darker than wine are his sparkling eyes,
      and his gleaming teeth are whiter than milk.

Zebulun dwells beside the seashore;
      his sheltered coast is a haven for ships,
      and his flank touches the border of Sidon.

Issachar is a strong-boned ass;
      between the sheepfolds he lies and rests.

When he saw how good his resting-place was,
    how green and fertile was all the land,
he bent his shoulder to carry loads
    and took forced burdens upon his back.

Dan rules over his people: small
    but equal to any of Israel's tribes.
Dan is a serpent by the side of the road,
    a poisonous viper along the path,
which darts out and bites the horse's fetlock
    and the horse's rider is thrown to the ground.

Gad is raided by nomad bands,
    but *his* bands ride out, raiding them back.

Asher, teeming with the richest of foods,
    grows delicacies that are fit for a king.

Naphtali is a swift-footed deer on the heights,
    who gives birth to fawns as beautiful as she.

Joseph is a young bull beside a well,
    a wild colt drinking from a desert spring.
Archers attacked him, shot at him, harried him,
    but his hands stayed firm and his bow stayed taut.
May God Almighty bless you
    with the blessings of the sky above,
    the blessings of the waters below,
the blessings of breasts and womb,
    the blessings of grain and blossom,
the blessings of the ancient mountains,
    the bounty of the timeless hills.
May these come to rest upon Joseph's head,
    and among his brothers may he stand alone.

Benjamin is a ravening wolf;
in the morning he kills and devours his prey;
at night he returns to divide the spoil.

(editorial addition:) These are the twelve tribes of Israel, and this is what their father said to them.

JACOB'S DEATH AND BURIAL (P) [49:1a, 28b-33, 50:12-13]

And Jacob sent for his sons, and he blessed them, with a special blessing for each. And he gave them these instructions: "I am about to be gathered to my ancestors. Bury me beside my fathers in the cave that is on the land of Ephron the Hittite, the cave of Machpelah, to the east of Mamre, in Canaan, which Abraham bought from Ephron the Hittite as a burial site. There Abraham and his wife Sarah were buried; there Isaac and his wife Rebecca were buried; and there I buried Leah." Then he drew his feet up onto the bed and died and was gathered to his ancestors.

And his sons did as he had instructed them: they brought him to Canaan and buried him in the cave of Machpelah, to the east of Mamre, which Abraham had bought as a burial site from Ephron the Hittite.

JOSEPH AND HIS BROTHERS RECONCILED (A LATER VERSION: R?) [50:15-21]

And when Joseph's brothers realized that their father was dead, they said, "What if Joseph still bears a grudge against us and takes revenge on us for all the harm we did to him?" So they sent this message to Joseph: "Your father gave us this message before he died: 'Say this to Joseph: "Forgive, I beg you, the crime and sin of your brothers, who did you harm."' So now, please, forgive the crime of the servants of the God of your father." And Joseph wept at their words to him.

Then his brothers themselves went and prostrated themselves before him and said, "We are ready to be your slaves."

And Joseph said to them, "Don't be afraid. Am I God? Besides, although you meant to harm me, God meant to bring good out of it: to save many lives, as we see today. So don't be afraid. I will take care of you and your children." Thus he reassured them and spoke kindly to them.

EPILOGUE (VERSION I: LATE SOURCE) [50:22-23]

So Joseph and his father's household remained in Egypt. And Joseph lived to be a hundred and ten years old. And he lived to see Ephraim's great-grandchildren. And he adopted the sons of Machir, Manasseh's son.

EPILOGUE (VERSION 2: LATE SOURCE) [50:24-26]

And Joseph said to his brothers, "I am about to die. But God will surely come to your rescue and take you up out of this land to the land that he swore to Abraham, to Isaac, and to Jacob." And he said, "When God comes to your rescue, you must take my bones with you to Canaan." And he made the sons of Israel swear it to him.

So Joseph died at the age of a hundred and ten, and he was embalmed and laid in a coffin in Egypt.

< APPENDIX 2 >

Appendix 2: The Flood [6:5–9:17]
[Roman – J; San Serif – J¹; *Italic – P; San Serif Italic – R*]

Now when the Lord saw how great the evil of humans was, and how every impulse in their hearts was nothing but evil all the time, he was sorry that he had made humans on the earth, and he was pained in his heart. And he said, "I will destroy all humankind from the earth: I am sorry I ever made them." But Noah found favor with the Lord.

This is the story of Noah. Noah was a righteous man, the one blameless man in that age. Noah walked with God. And Noah had three sons: Shem, Ham, and Japheth.

And the earth was exceedingly corrupt and filled with violence. And when God saw how corrupt the earth was and how corrupt humankind had become on the earth, God said to Noah, "I am going to put an end to humankind, for the earth is filled with violence because of them: I am going to blot them out from the earth. Make yourself an ark of cypress wood; cover it with reeds and caulk it inside and outside with pitch. Make it with lower, second, and third decks. And this is how you should make it: the ark should be five hundred feet long, one hundred feet wide, and fifty feet high. Make a skylight for the ark, and finish it two feet from the top. And put an entrance to the ark in its longer side.

"I am going to bring a great flood onto the earth, to exterminate all living creatures: everything on earth will perish. But I promise to rescue you; you will go into the ark, you and your sons and your wife and your sons' wives with you. And you will take one pair of every kind of creature, male and female, into the ark to stay alive with you. One pair of every kind of bird, animal, and reptile will come to you, to stay alive. And you will take with you all the food that you need, and store it away, to serve as food for you and for them." And Noah did everything God had commanded.

< APPENDIX 2 >

And the Lord said to Noah, "Go into the ark, with all your household; for you alone I have found righteous in this age. Take with you seven pairs, male and female, of all the clean animals, and one pair, male and female, of all the unclean animals, *and also seven pairs, male and female, of all the birds,* to make sure that life continues on the earth. Seven days from now, I will make it rain on the earth for forty days and forty nights; and I will destroy from the earth every creature that I made." And Noah did as the Lord had commanded him.

And Noah was six hundred years old when the flood came onto the earth. And Noah, *and his sons and his wife and his sons' wives with him,* went into the ark, because of the great flood. *One pair, male and female, of all the clean animals, all the unclean animals, and all the birds, and of every creature on earth came into the ark with Noah, as God had commanded Noah.*

And after seven days, the waters of the flood came onto the earth. *And in the six hundredth year of Noah's life, in the second month, on the seventeenth day of the month, all the wells of the great deep burst, and the floodgates of heaven opened.* And the rain fell onto the earth for forty days and forty nights. *On that day Noah, and Shem, Ham, and Japheth, Noah's sons, and Noah's wife, and the three wives of his sons with them, went into the ark, and with them every kind of animal, reptile, and bird: one pair of every creature went into the ark with Noah, a male and a female, as God had commanded him.* And the Lord shut the door behind him. *And the flood came down onto the earth for forty days,* and the waters rose and lifted the ark above the earth. *And the waters rose higher above the earth, and the ark drifted on the waters. And the waters rose higher and higher above the earth, until they covered the highest mountains under heaven. Thirty feet above the mountains the waters rose. And all creatures on earth perished—all birds and all animals and all reptiles and all humans.* Everything that had the breath of life in its nostrils, everything on the dry land, died; he destroyed every creature on earth, *humans and animals and reptiles and birds of the sky;* they were completely destroyed. And only Noah was left, and those who were with him in the ark.

And when the waters had risen above the earth for a hundred and fifty days,

God remembered Noah and all the creatures that were with him in the ark. And God swept a wind over the earth, and the waters stopped rising. And the wells of the deep and the floodgates of heaven were shut, and the rain was held back from heaven. And the waters stopped rising above the earth, *and at the end of the hundred and fifty days the waters began to subside. And in the seventh month, on the seventeenth day of the month, the ark came to rest on the mountains of Ararat. And the waters kept subsiding until the tenth month: in the tenth month, on the first day of the month, the tops of the mountains appeared.*

And at the end of forty days Noah opened the window he had made in the ark, and he sent out a raven, and it flew back and forth, until the waters had dried up from the ground. And he sent out a dove, to see if the waters had subsided. But the dove found no place where her feet could settle, because the waters still covered the whole earth, and she returned to the ark. And Noah put out his hand and took her and brought her into the ark.

And he waited seven more days. And again he sent out the dove from the ark. And toward evening the dove came back to him, and there in her beak was a freshly plucked olive leaf, and Noah knew that the waters had subsided.

And he waited seven more days. And he sent out the dove. And she didn't return.

And in the six hundred and first year, in the first month, on the first day of the month, the waters began to dry from the earth. And Noah took off the ark's cover and looked out, and indeed the ground was dry. *And in the second month, on the twenty-seventh day of the month, the earth was dry.*

And God said to Noah, "Come out of the ark, you and your wife and your sons and your sons' wives with you. And bring out every creature that is with you, every bird, animal, and reptile, and let them be fruitful and multiply and spread over all the earth."

And Noah came out, and his sons and his wife and his sons' wives with him. And every creature, every animal, bird, and reptile, group by group, came out of the ark.

And Noah built an altar to the Lord, and he took one of every clean animal and bird and offered them as sacrifices on the altar. And the Lord smelled the soothing odor and said to himself, "Never again will I curse the ground because of humans, however evil the impulse of the human heart may be, and never again will I strike down all living things as I have done. For as long as the earth endures, these will not end: seedtime and harvest, cold and heat, summer and winter, day and night."

And God blessed Noah and his sons, saying, "Be fruitful and multiply, and replenish the earth. And the fear of you will fall on every animal, every bird, every creature on earth, and every fish in the sea: they are all in your power. Every creature that moves will be yours to eat; I give them all to you, just as I gave you the green plants. But you must not eat flesh from a still-living animal. And I will require an accounting for the death of every human: I will require it from every animal, and I will require it from every human. Whoever sheds human blood, his blood will be shed; for in his own image did God make humans."

And God said to Noah and to his sons, "For your part, be fruitful and multiply; spread over the earth and rule it. For my part, I now make a solemn promise to you and to your offspring after you and to every creature that was with you, all birds and animals and reptiles that came out of the ark. And I will keep my promise to you: never again will all creatures be destroyed by the waters of a flood, and never again will there be a flood to blot out the earth."

And God said, "This is the sign of the promise that I make to you and to every living creature that was with you, for all ages to come: I am setting my rainbow in the clouds, and it will be the sign of my promise to the earth. And whenever I bring clouds over the earth and the rainbow appears in the clouds, I will remember my promise to you and to every creature, and the waters will never again become a flood to blot out all life. And when the rainbow appears in the clouds, I will see it and remember the eternal promise I have made to every creature on earth."

And God said to Noah, "This is the sign of the promise that I have established for every creature on earth."

< APPENDIX 3 >

Appendix 3: The Rape of Dinah [34:1–31, 35:5]

[Roman – A version; San Serif – B version; *San Serif Italic – C version*]

Now Dinah, the daughter whom Leah had borne to Jacob, went out to visit some women of that region. And when Shechem, son of Hamor the Hivite, ruler of the region, saw her, he took her and slept with her by force. And he fell in love with Dinah, and he spoke kindly to her and tried to win her heart. And he said to his father Hamor, "Get me this girl as my wife."

And Jacob heard that Shechem had violated his daughter Dinah. But since his sons were out with the livestock in the open country, Jacob did nothing until they returned. And when his sons heard what had happened, they came back, and they were outraged, because he had committed an outrage in Israel by sleeping with Jacob's daughter, a thing not to be done.

Then Shechem's father Hamor came out to Jacob to talk the matter over with him. And he said, "My son Shechem is in love with your daughter. Please give her to him as his wife, and make a marriage alliance with us: give us your daughters and take our daughters for yourselves. And live among us, settle in our land, move around freely in it, and acquire property."

And Shechem said to her father and brothers, "Do me this favor, and I will pay whatever you ask. Name as high a bride-price as you want and I will pay it. Just give me the girl as my wife."

And Jacob's sons answered *Shechem and his father* Hamor, *and they spoke deceitfully, because he had violated their sister Dinah,* "We can't give our sister to a man who is uncircumcised — that is a disgrace among us. Only on one condition will we consent: if every male among you is circumcised as we are. Then we will give you our daughters, and we will take your daughters for ourselves, and we will live with you and become one people. But if you don't agree to be circumcised, we will take our sister [Hebrew Text: daughter] and go."

And their request seemed fair to Hamor and Hamor's son Shechem. **And the young man lost no time in doing what they had said, because he greatly desired Jacob's daughter. (He was the most respected man in his father's household.)**

And Hamor and his son Shechem went to the city council and said to the men of the city, "These men have come to us in peace. Let them settle in our land and move around freely in it: the land is large enough to include them. We will take their daughters as wives and give them our daughters. But the men will consent to live with us and become one people only on this condition: that every male among us be circumcised, as they are. Won't their cattle, their possessions, and all their animals be advantageous for us? Let us agree to their terms, so that they will settle among us."

And all the able-bodied men of the city agreed with Hamor and his son Shechem, and every male in the city was circumcised [Septuagint (ancient Greek translation): on the flesh of his foreskin]. **And on the third day, when they were still in pain, two of Jacob's sons, Simeon and Levi, Dinah's full brothers, took their swords and entered the city unopposed. And they cut down** *Hamor and his son* **Shechem and took Dinah from Shechem's house and left.** The sons of Jacob attacked the ailing men [reading *haḥōlîm*] [25: *and killed every male*] and plundered the city, because their sister had been violated. They took their sheep, their oxen, their donkeys, everything inside the city and outside it, all their wealth; and they took all their children and women as slaves [Hebrew Text: and plundered everything in the house].

Then Jacob said to Simeon and Levi, "You have stirred up trouble for me and made me hateful to the people of this region, *the Canaanites and the Perizzites.* **And since my numbers are few, they will join forces and attack me, and I will be destroyed, with all my family."**

And they said, "Should we let our sister be treated like a whore?"

And they departed. And a great terror fell on the cities all around, and none of them pursued the sons of Jacob.

BIBLIOGRAPHY
AND NOTES

<SELECTED BIBLIOGRAPHY>

Selected Bibliography

Ehrlich, Arnold B. *Randglossen zur Hebräischen Bibel, Band 1*. Leipzig, 1908.

Elliger, K., W. Rudolf, et al. *Biblia Hebraica Stuttgartensia*. Stuttgart, 1983.

Gunkel, Hermann. *Genesis*. Göttingen, 1901.

Sarna, Nahum N. *The JPS Torah Commentary: Genesis*. Philadelphia, 1989.

Skinner, John. *A Critical and Exegetical Commentary on Genesis*. New York, 1910.

Speiser, E. A. *Genesis*. Garden City, N. Y., 1964.

Westermann, Claus. *Genesis 1-11: A Commentary*, trans. John J. Scullion, S.J. Minneapolis, 1984.

Westermann, Claus. *Genesis 12-36: A Commentary*, trans. John J. Scullion, S.J. Minneapolis, 1985.

Westermann, Claus. *Genesis 37-50: A Commentary*, trans. John J. Scullion, S.J. Minneapolis, 1986.

I have also consulted *The Revised English Bible*, Oxford, 1989; James Moffatt, *A New Translation of the Bible*, New York, 1934; and Robert Graves and Raphael Patai, *Hebrew Myths: The Book of Genesis*, Garden City, N.Y., 1964. I have learned from all three and have occasionally appropriated a word or a phrase.

Textual and Philological Notes

I am deeply indebted to the great three-volume commentary on Genesis by Claus Westermann, and also to Arnold B. Ehrlich's *Randglossen zur Hebräischen Bibel.*

I have left unmentioned any minor textual corrections that didn't affect the meaning of a verse.

ABBREVIATIONS

𝔄	Arabic version	𝔖	Peshitta (Syriac version)
BHS	*Biblia Hebraica Stuttgartensia*	𝔗	Targum (Aramaic version)
ℭ	manuscript from the Cairo Geniza	𝔙	Vulgate (Jerome's Latin version)
cj.	conjecture	Θ	Theodotion (Greek version)
𝔎	Coptic version	Σ	Symmachus (Greek version)
𝔏	Latin version	ᴟ	Samaritan version
LXX	Septuagint (Greek version)	>	lacking in
MT	Massoretic Text		

THE CREATION (ACCORDING TO P)

1:6   *lmym* Insert *wyhy kn* from v. 7 (LXX).

1:7   *lrqy'* Insert *wayyar' 'lōhîm kî ṭôb* (cf. LXX).

1:20   *hšmym* Insert *wyhy kn* (LXX).

1:26   *h'rṣ* Insert *ḥayyat* (𝔖; cf. vv. 24, 25).

2:4a   Omitted (from R):

That is the story of how heaven and earth were created.

THE CREATION (ACCORDING TO J)

2:4b   *yhwh 'lhym* Read *yhwh*. "The double name has sometimes been explained by the supposition that an editor added *'lhym* to the original *yhwh* in order to smooth the transition from P to J. . . . [Another theory assumes] that two closely parallel accounts existed, one of which (Jᵉ) employed only *'lhym*, the other (Jʲ) only *yhwh*. When these were combined the editor harmonised them by adding *'lhym* to *yhwh* everywhere in J^j, and prefixing *yhwh* to *'lhym* everywhere in J^e except in the colloquy between the serpent and the woman (3:1-5), where the general name was felt to be more appropriate" (Skinner).

2:8b   Omitted: doublet of 15. I have combined the verses.

2:10-14   Omitted (later addition):

> A river arises from Eden to water the garden, and from there it divides into four. The name of the first is Pishon, and it winds through the whole land of Havilah, where the gold is. (The gold of that land is good; there is fine resin there, and onyx.) And the name of the second river is Gihon, and it winds through the whole land of Ethiopia. And the name of the third river is Tigris, and it flows east of Asshur. And the fourth river is Euphrates.

2:19   *npš ḥyh*   Delete: gloss (BHS).

2:20   *wl'dm*   Point *wᵉlā'ādām* (BHS).

2:21   "Job 4:13, as well as Dan. 8:18 and 10:9, might fairly serve as proof that the specific meaning 'prophetic ecstasy, vision' which was attributed to the word *trdmh* is still traceable as far back as the Hebrew linguistic consciousness of late-biblical times" (I. L. Seeligmann, *The Septuagint Version of Isaiah*, Leiden, 1948, p. 53, q.v. for the biblical and midrashic evidence; also Fullerton, *Journal of Biblical Literature* 49, 347). Here and in 15:12 *trdmh* is translated by LXX as *ekstasis* and "evidently conceived as meaning a prophetic exaltation."

3:2   *mpry 'ṣ*   Read *mpry kol-'ṣ* (𝔖) or *mikol-'ṣ* (LXX).

3:6   *wnḥmd h'ṣ lhśkyl*   The usual translation, "the tree was desirable for acquiring wisdom," is too complicated a thought for J's beautifully simple style in the Eden story. That the tree conferred knowledge is what the woman heard from the serpent, not something she could actually see. Textually, it is suspicious that the subject is repeated here and that the clause is not introduced by *ky* as the first two parallel clauses are. "In this context it is more accurate to translate, with LXX, Peshitta, and Vulgate, 'that the tree was lovely to contemplate'; the clause is parallel to 'that it was a pleasure for the eyes' and no doubt just a manuscript variant" (Gunkel).

3:10   *w'yr'*   Read *wā'ēre'* (MS, 𝔖).

3:16   *whrnk*   Read *wᵉhegyônēk* (LXX).

        tšwqtk   "That *tšwqtk* does not mean 'desire' is clear from the context here and especially 4:7. In both places the noun clearly indicates the relationship of a person to another who rules over him. Such a relationship is not at all identical with desire.... The most likely sense is arrived at by comparing *tšwqtk* with Arabic *s'q*, but not accepting that the sense of 'to drive' is fundamental to the meaning of the noun. *s'q* II means to hand over one's things to the discretion of someone else, to submit them to him, from which concept comes the meaning *swqh*, subjection, in a concrete sense. Hence *tšwqtk*, a noun form that corresponds to the hitpael of the verb, can very well mean *submission*. This fits excellently here and in 4:7; cf. 41:40 and Song of Songs 7:11" (Ehrlich).

3:17   Omitted (later addition):
        In pain you shall eat it / all the days of your life.

3:18   Omitted (later addition):
        ... and you shall eat the plants of the field.

3:24   *hkrbym*   I have used the transliteration *kerub* here, since *cherub* unavoidably evokes images of rosy-cheeked infant-angels. The *kerubim* are apparently huge winged creatures, possibly equivalent to the Akkadian *kuribu*, human-headed bulls with eagles' wings. Ezekiel, on the other hand, describes them as each having four faces (human, lion, bull, eagle), four wings, human hands, a body "gleaming like polished bronze," and calves' feet.

CAIN AND ABEL (J)

4:1   *knyty*   With the meaning "to create," the verb usually has God as its subject (Gen. 14:19, 22, Ex. 15:16, Deut. 32:6, Ps. 78:54, 139:13, Prov. 8:22).

       't   This seems to have the sense of "together with, as well as, equally with." "A strikingly similar phrase in the bilingual Babylonian account of Creation suggests that the language here may be more deeply tinged with mythology than has been generally suspected: 'Aruru, together with him (Marduk), created (the) seed of mankind'... The exclamation certainly gains in significance if we suppose it to have survived from a more mythological phase of tradition, in which *Hawwah* was not a mortal wife and mother, but a creative deity taking part with the supreme god in the production of man" (Skinner).

Ehrlich's treatment is attractive, though it requires an emendation: "In the second half of the verse all the commentators, ancient as well as modern, read *'yš* as referring to Cain, but contrary to usage. For if even the three-month-old Moses in Ex. 2:6 is called *n'r*, here *'yš* cannot possibly refer to the newly-born Cain. *'yš* always means a grown man.... Here it can refer only to Adam. Eve does not say *'yšy* because by *'yš* no other man can be understood except Adam, since no other man exists. In this context *qnh* means *to win back*; cf. the use of *bnh* in Ps. 122:3 in the sense of 'to rebuild.' Finally, *'itti* should be read for *'t*; the *yod* dropped out through haplography. The words in question thus form two short clauses. The first one, in which the perfect tense indicates an action to be awaited with certainty, means: 'I will win back my husband,' and the second one: 'YHVH is with me.' Eve has through her error incurred YHVH's wrath and also forfeited the affection of her husband, whom she drew with her into ruin. Now, in the birth of her first son, she sees not only a joyous event that will win her back the heart of her husband, but also a sign that YHVH has forgiven her sin and once more is with her."

4:6–7 Omitted (later addition):

> And the Lord said to Cain, "Why are you troubled, and why has your face fallen? If you bear this well (?) . . . ; but if you don't (bear it?), [the next phrase is unintelligible]. And he will be subject to you, and you will rule over him."

"The closing words are taken from 3:16: 'Its desire is for you, but you must master it.' H. Ewald has already observed correctly that the quotation of the words from 3:16 in 4:7 is artificial and mechanical, whereas the trial and the sentence of Gen. 4 echo Gen. 3 naturally and organically. This mechanical citation which gives the words a quite different meaning in the new context . . . is the surest sign that 4:6–7 must be a subsequent addition or modification. It has even been suggested that the sentence is really a gloss to 3:16 which has found its way into the text in the wrong place" (Westermann).

4:7a This verse is unintelligible; J's simple and lucid style could not possibly result in the muddle of MT, with its mini-allegory of Sin lurking as a demon at the door. "All explanations or attempts at emendation of the text have failed. It must be admitted that the text is very corrupt" (Westermann).

4:8   *ḥyw* Insert *nēlkâ haśśādeh* (𝔪, LXX, 𝔖, 𝔏, 𝔙).

       bśdh "It is clear that this word, in connection with an event from primeval time, when all land on earth was nothing but fields, should not be understood literally. *śdh* in opposition to *ʿyr* designates a remote place where there are no passersby, then particularly circumstances in which a cry for help does no good, since no one is likely to hear it (cf. Deut. 22:25-27). Hence *bhywtm bśdh* here = when they were quite alone, away from their parents" (Ehrlich).

4:14   *mpnyk ʾstr* "This expression occurs only here and in Job 13:20, where fortunately its sense is clear from the context. There the hero gives God two conditions, the granting of which will take away all his fear, and adds *ʾz mpnyk lʾ ʾstr*, which can only mean 'then I will not lay down my arms before you,' more literally 'then I will not creep away before you.' And this, mutatis mutandis, fits excellently here. *mpnyk ʾstr* thus means 'and I must stoop before you, must submit to your judgment.' Hence Cain's fear does not arise from the consciousness that from now on he will be deprived of God's protection, but from the consciousness of having no home. The homeless man, the vagabond, has been hated from time immemorial, and everywhere he goes he runs the danger of misunderstanding and suspicion" (Ehrlich).

4:15   *lkn* Read *lōʾ kēn* (LXX, Σ, Θ, 𝔖, 𝔙).

SETH; THE DESCENDANTS OF CAIN (J)

4:17   *kśm bnw* Read *kiśᵉmô* (cj. Budde).

4:22   *twbl qyn* Read *tûbal* (LXX).

       lṭś Insert *ʾᵃbî kol-* (𝔗).

4:25-26   Insert after v. 16.

       ʾḥr tḥt hbl ky hrgw qyn Delete: gloss. I have retained *ʾḥr* in the translation for the sake of clarity.

GENEALOGIES (P)

5:22   *ʾt hʾlhym* Insert *wayᵉḥî ḥᵃnôk* (LXX^min [𝔙^MSS]).

5:29   Insert after 4:18. "This verse is almost universally ascribed to J.... The appearance of Noah at the end of Gen. 5 gives reason to presume a previous stage of the sequence in 4:17-18 that included Noah. One can more readily accept this because with Lamech in 4:19 there begins another tradition that did not originally belong in the sequence 4:17-18" (Westermann).

ynḥmnw Read *yᵉniḥēnû* (LXX). "Here *hēniaḥ* means *to give pleasure and ease; see* Pr. 29:17. In *mm'śnw* and *m'ṣbwn ydynw* the preposition means *after* (cf. Jg. 11:4 and Hos. 6:2); on the other hand, the third *mn* indicates the source of the pleasure" (Ehrlich).

THE GODS AND THE WOMEN (J)

6:3   I have omitted this very obscure verse, since it is out of place in its present context:

> And the Lord said, "My breath (spirit) will not continue (?) in man forever, since he too (?) is flesh; let the time allowed him be a hundred and twenty years."

6:4   *wgm 'ḥry kn* Delete. "Probably added by an anxious reader who knew that giants still existed in later times" (Gunkel); cf. Num. 13:33, Deut. 3:11, Josh. 13:12, etc.

THE FLOOD (ACCORDING TO J AND TO P)

6:5ff.   These verses are generally attributed to the following sources — J: 6:5-8, 7:1-5, 7, 10, 12, 16b, 17b, 22-23, 8:2b-3a, 6-12, 13b, 20-22; P: 6:9-22, 7:6, 11, 13-16a, 17a, 18-21, 24, 8:1-2a, 3b-5, 13a, 14-19, 9:1-17; R: 7:8-9.

6:7   *'šr br'ty* Delete (from R).

        m'dm 'd bhmh 'd rmś w'd 'wp hšmym Delete (from R).

6:11-12   *kl bśr* For the meaning "humanity," see Westermann, ad loc.

6:13   *'t* Read *mē'ēt* (cj. Graetz: haplography; BHS: ?) or *mē'al* (cj. Olshausen).

6:14   *qnym* Point *qānîm* (G. R. Driver, *Vetus Testamentum* 4 [1954], 243).

6:17   *mym* Delete: gloss (BHS).

7:3a   Omitted (from R):

> ... and seven pairs, male and female, of all the birds ...

7:6   Omitted (from P or R):

> And Noah was six hundred years old when the flood came onto the earth.

7:7ff. Scholars are generally agreed that the order of the verses from J is as follows: 7:10, 7, 16b, 12, 17b, 22–23, 8:6a, 2b, 3a, 6b–12.

7:8-9 Omitted (from R):

> One pair, male and female, of all the clean animals and of all the animals that are not clean, of all the birds, and of every creature on earth came into the ark with Noah, as the Lord had commanded.

7:14 *kl ṣpwr kl knp* Delete: gloss (> LXX).

7:17 *'rb'ym ywm* Delete: gloss.

7:22-23 I have followed Gunkel's suggestion that the original sequence was 23a, 22, 23c.

7:23 Omitted (from R):

> . . . humans and animals and reptiles and birds of the sky . . .

8:3 *m'l* Read *'al* (Ehrlich: dittography).

8:7 Omitted (variant):

> And he sent out a raven, and it flew back and forth, until the waters had dried up from the ground.

9:7 *wrbw* Read *ûr^{e}dû* (LXX^{L}; cf. 1:28).

9:10 *lkl ḥyt h'rṣ* Delete: gloss (>LXX).

9:15–16 *bkl-bśr* Delete: gloss.

9:17 Omitted:

> And God said to Noah, "This is the sign of the promise that I have established for every creature on earth."

NOAH'S DRUNKENNESS (J)

9:18 *wḥm hw' 'by kn'n* Delete: gloss.

9:26 *brwk yhwh 'lhy šm* Read *bārēk yhwh 'oholê šm* (cj. Graetz).

GENEALOGIES (P,J)

9:28ff. These verses are generally attributed to the following sources— P: 9:28, 10:1–7, 20, 22–23, 31–32; J: 10:8–19, 21, 24–30.

10:4 *wddnym* Read *w^{e}rōdānîm* (𝔪, LXX, 1 Chron 1:7).

10:5 *hgwym* Insert *'ēlleh b^{e}nê yepet* (cf. vv. 20, 31).

10:8 *lpny yhwh* This phrase is "a form of the superlative" (B. Jacob); I have left it untranslated.

10:14 *w't kptrym* Insert after *kslḥym*.

THE TOWER OF BABEL (J)

11:3-4   I have transposed these two verses.

11:4   *šm* Point *šām* (Ehrlich). " *'šh l* should be understood with the sense that it has in 30:30 and *šm* should be pointed *šām*. The following clause depends on *wn'šh lnw šām*, and the whole clause means 'and there we will provide for ourselves — literally, care for ourselves — so that we are not etc.' For the expression, cf. my commentary on Josh. 22:26. *šēm* cannot be correct, because the whole of humanity existing at that time is speaking and it would therefore be impossible to understand among whom the speakers wish to make themselves famous. For primitive humanity could hardly be thinking of fame among their posterity. Also, the content of the second half-verse shows that with this enterprise they are thinking of the present, and not of the future" (Ehrlich).

11:5   I have omitted *yrd* in this verse: here the Lord descends to earth, yet in v. 7 he *decides* to descend to earth. The two incompatible phrases come from two different sources that J has combined.

11:8   I have transposed 8a and 8b.

GENEALOGIES (P)

11:28-30   These verses are generally attributed to J.

11:31   *wyṣ'w* Read *wayyēṣē'* (𝕾ʷ) or *wayyōṣē'* [*'ōtām*] (𝔪, LXX, 𝖁).

THE PROMISE TO ABRAM (J)

12:3   *wmqllk* Read *ûmᵉqalᵉlékā* (ℂ, 𝔪, LXX, 𝕾, 𝖁).

   wnbrkw bk kl mšpḥt h'dmh The expression can also mean "and all the peoples of the earth will wish themselves blessed like you" or "will bless one another in you," i.e., "the peoples of the earth will in their blessings name Abraham as the paradigm of a man who is blessed and fortunate" (Ehrlich).

12:4b-5   Omitted (from P):

   And Abram was seventy-five years old when he left Haran. And Abram took Sarai his wife, and Lot his brother's son, and all their possessions that they had obtained, and the people that they had acquired in Haran, and they set out for the land of Canaan, [and they arrived in Canaan].

WIFE AND SISTER (VERSION I: J)

12:17 *w't bytw* Delete: gloss.

ABRAM AND LOT (J)

13:5 *w'hlym* Read *ûgᵉmallîm* (cj. Ehrlich). "Tents are never named in the Hebrew Bible as a component of wealth or possessions."

13:6, 11b-12bα Omitted (from P):

> And the land could not contain them if they stayed together, for their possessions were great, and they could not stay together. So they separated from each other; Abram settled in the land of Canaan, and Lot settled among the cities of the plain.

13:13 Omitted (later addition):

> Now the people of Sodom were wicked and sinned against the Lord very greatly.

ABRAM AND THE KINGS (LATE REDACTOR, USING THREE EARLY SOURCES)

14:1ff. There is general scholarly agreement that this chapter is an inept patchwork of three separate parts: A. The campaign against the rebel kings (vv. 1-11, with an independent document, vv. 5b-7, spliced onto it); B. The rescue of Lot (vv. 12-17, 21-24); C. The blessing by Melchizedek (vv. 18-20). "Part B forms the basic material into which C was later inserted; A was then prefixed to the composite B and C, and consequently determined the whole. . . . The narrative 14:12-24 (without the name Abraham) originated in the period of the judges and comes from a cycle of savior narratives. . . . The addition (vv. 18-20) very probably arose in the time of David; an experience of Abraham is narrated with the purpose of legitimating cultic innovations of that period. The report of the campaign (vv. 1-11) with its many names is certainly of extra-Israelite origin; it follows in style and structure the royal inscriptions of Assyrian-Babylonian kings. The manner of presentation is unhistorical despite the acknowledgment of a historical document which lies behind it; the lists of names are joined to the report of the campaign in a clumsy way. The composite text of vv. 1-11 and 12-24 is the work of a scribe's desk from the late postexilic period, to be compared with other late Jewish writings" (Westermann).

14:6   *bhrrm*   Read *bᵉharᵉrê* (𝔐, LXX, 𝔖, 𝔙).

14:14   *wyrq*   Read *wayyādeq* (𝔐, LXX, 𝔙).

THE PROMISE TO ABRAM: DESCENDANTS (LATE SOURCE)

15:1   *mgn*   Point *mōgēn* (Ehrlich; cf. 14:20).

15:2   *hw' dmśq* is an obvious gloss for the obscure *bn mśq*; but the entire half-verse is obscure. I have translated the equivalent phrase from v. 3.

15:3   Delete: gloss.

THE PROMISE TO ABRAM: LAND (LATE SOURCE)

15:7   "A redactor altered the introduction in v. 7 to *wy'mr 'lyw* to make vv. 7-21 a continuation of vv. 1-6" (Westermann).

15:9   "*mślś* and *mślśt* describe animals from the third litter of their mother. The third litter was especially valued; cf. *'gl' tylt'* Sabbath 11a. Pesachim 68b and see Rashi ad loc" (Ehrlich).

15:12   *ḥśkh*   Delete: gloss (BHS: ?).

15:13-16   Omitted (later addition):

> And he said to Abram, "Know well that your offspring will be aliens in a land that is not theirs; and they will enslave them and oppress them for four hundred years. And I will also judge that nation to whom they are enslaved. And afterward they will come out with great wealth. And as for you, you will go to your fathers in peace; you will be buried at a ripe old age. And they will return here in the fourth generation, for the iniquity of the Amorites is not yet complete."

15:19-21   Omitted (later addition):

> . . . the Kenites, the Kenizzites, the Kadmonites, the Hittites, the Perizzites, the Rephaites, the Amorites, the Canaanites, the Girgashites, and the Jebusites.

HAGAR AND ISHMAEL (ACCORDING TO J)

16:1   "Hagar is not an ordinary household slave, but the peculiar property of Sarai, and therefore not at the free disposal of her master" (Skinner).

16:3   Omitted (from P):

And Abram's wife Sarai took Hagar the Egyptian, her maid, after
Abram had lived ten years in the land of Canaan, and gave her to
Abram her husband as his concubine.

16:7, 11 *ml'k yhwh* "The basic sense of *mal'ak*, the Hebrew word rendered
ángelos, is 'Presence.' As applied to God himself appearing to men,
this presence may be called 'manifestation.' As applied to messengers sent to men by other men or by God, this *praesent-ia* can be called
re-praesent-atio, a vicarious presence or manifestation of a different
type.... It seems inescapable that the *mal'ak yhwh* is in some cases an
expression for God himself. When it is God, this fact is known only
because it speaks as God, not from any description of its external
appearance or activities, or of its nature: it is a superhuman being, but
not an angel or messenger at all" (Robert North, *Catholic Biblical
Quarterly* 29 [1967], 419-449).

That the character here is God rather than an angel is clear from v.
13, where Hagar acknowledges that she spoke with and saw the Lord
himself. Compare the following passages: in 21:17ff. the *malakh elohim*
says, "I will make him into a great nation"; in 31:11ff. the *malakh ha-elohim* says, "I am the God of Beth-El"; in 48:15f. Israel uses God and
malakh as parallel words ("the God who has been my shepherd all my
life, to this day" = "the *malakh* who has rescued me from all harm").
yhwh is also interchangeable with *malakh yhwh* in Ex. 3:2 and 3:4, and
with *malakh ha-elohim* in Ex. 14:19 and 14:24.

16:9-10 Omitted (later addition):
And the Lord [*ml'k yhwh*] said to her, "Go back to your mistress,
and submit to her harsh treatment." And the Lord [*ml'k yhwh*] said
to her, "I will multiply your descendants very greatly, and they will
be too many to be counted."

16:12 *pr' 'dm* "Dahood (*Catholic Biblical Quarterly* 25 [1963], 123f.) has shown
that *'dm* is sometimes equivalent to *'dmh*, 'ground.' Accordingly, *pr' 'dm*
would mean 'a wild ass of the steppe'" (M. H. Pope, *Job*, Garden City,
N.Y., 1965, 1973, ad 11:12).

16:13 *'th* (= *'ittāh*) Delete: gloss to *'lyh* (Ehrlich).
'l r'y "This means 'a God of seeing,' in other words, 'a God who can be
seen'" (Ehrlich).

ḥlm r'yty Read *'ĕlohîm rā'îtî wā'eḥî* (cj. Wellhausen). In the interpretation of this phrase and of *b'r lḥy r'y* in the following verse, I have followed Ehrlich.

16:15-16 Omitted (from P):

> And Hagar bore Abram a son; and Abram named the son that Hagar bore Ishmael. And Abram was eighty-six years old when Hagar bore Ishmael to Abram.

ABRAHAM AND THE THREE VISITORS (J)

18:2 *'nšym* In chapters 18 and 19, *'nšym* means "non-human men, supernatural beings"; the category includes YHVH here, as does *'yš* in 32:25.

18:5 *kn t'śh k'šr dbrt* "The phrase can have no other meaning than this: 'Do just as you have said', i. e., 'We will accept your hospitality only under the condition that, as you have promised, you won't make too much of an effort or provide us with too elaborate a meal.' This extremely courteous speech can only belong to a very much later time" (Ehrlich).

18:7 "*k't ḥyh* indicates the passage not of a full year but of only nine months, the time of pregnancy; cf. 2 Kings 4:16f." (Ehrlich).

ABRAHAM QUESTIONS THE DESTRUCTION OF SODOM (LATE SOURCE)

18:19 *yd'tyw* Point *yiddā'tîw* and cf. Job 38:12 (Ehrlich).

18:21 *klh* Read *kūllāh* (Wellhausen, BHS).

18:22 Insert after v. 19.

> *w'brhm . . . yhwh* This is one of the tiqqunê sopherim. Read *wyhwh . . . 'brhm*.

THE DESTRUCTION OF SODOM AND GOMORRAH (J)

19:12 *ḥtn* Delete: scribal error from v. 14.

> *wbnyk* Read *bānékā* (37 MSS, ш).

19:18-23,30 "This whole passage about Zoar is secondary. The statement in v. 31, 'there are no men left on earth to lie with us,' clearly shows that everything that is said about Zoar proceeds from a later hand. Only according to the original story, in which Lot fled directly from Sodom into the hills, can the daughters believe that the whole world had perished as in the Flood; they could not believe this, however, if they had

< NOTES >

in the meantime been living in Zoar and seen its inhabitants quite alive" (Ehrlich). The omitted passage reads as follows:

> And Lot said, "Please don't, sir. You have been so good to me and have shown me such great kindness in saving my life, but if I try to run to the hills, the destruction will overtake me and I will die. Look, that town over there, I can go to it, and it is so small. Please let me go there: it is so small, and my life will be saved." And he said to him, "I will grant you this favor too, and I will not obliterate the town. Hurry, go; for I can't do anything [or, reading *hadabar* with Ehrlich, I can't do the thing, i.e., I can't save it] until you get there." That is why the town was named Zoar, *Small*. The sun was rising as Lot entered Zoar. . . . And Lot went up from Zoar and lived in the hill country, for he was afraid to live in Zoar.

19:29   Omitted (from P):

> So it happened, after God destroyed the cities of the plain, that God, remembering Abraham, sent Lot out of the midst of the obliteration, when he obliterated the cities that Lot lived in.

WIFE AND SISTER (VERSION 2: E)

20:4   *hgwy gm* Read *hᵃgam* (cj. Ball: dittography).

20:6   "When God says, 'I have not allowed you to touch her,' this cannot mean a voluntary abstinence, but one imposed by God. It would be contrary to all experience that a middle-eastern king who had sent for a beautiful woman should voluntarily have conquered his sexual desire and kept the object of it for some time, or even for a single night, without touching her. In fact, God prevented him from touching Sarah by putting him in a condition that made the consummation of sexual intercourse impossible for him" (Ehrlich).

20:9b-10   Omitted:

> "You have done things to me that ought not to be done." And Abimelech said to Abraham, "What were you thinking of, that made you do this thing?"

20:16   *kswt 'ynym* Obscure. The sentence reads literally: "Let this be a covering for the eyes for everything that [or: to everyone who] is with you."

w't kl wnkḥt Read *we'at küllô nkḥt* (cj. Gunkel, BHS).

20:17bβ-18 Omitted (later addition):

> . . . and his wife and his concubines, and they gave birth to children. For the Lord had closed up all the wombs in the household of Abimelech, because of Sarah, Abraham's wife.

"It has already been shown how God made sure that Abimelech could not touch Sarah. Here this is clearly indicated by *wyrp'*, which would otherwise be inexplicable, since for the removal of sterility of the body only *pth rhm* can be used, and obviously just in relation to women. Here a reference to the removal of sterility of the body is not at issue, because the confirmation of this requires a longer period of time. . . . *wyldw* as well as the entire verse that follows is not part of the original text. v. 18 is easily recognizable as a later addition through its use of *yhwh* instead of the *'lhym* that is otherwise used through this episode. This addition, clear in itself, is inexplicable in its context" (Ehrlich).

THE FAMILY OF ABRAHAM (P,R, LATE SOURCE)

20:17bα After this verse I have inserted 21:1b, 2b-5 (P), 22:20-24 (R, P) and 25:1-4 (late source).

HAGAR AND ISHMAEL (ACCORDING TO E)

21:1a, 2a For the sake of clarity, I have introduced the story with these two half-verses from J, changing *yhwh* to *'lhym*.

21:1b Omitted (from J):

> . . . and the Lord did for Sarah as he had said.

21:6 This verse as well has been ascribed to J. Since it is an explanation of the name *yshk*, in its original setting it must have been preceded by "And she named him Isaac."

21:7 Omitted (from J):

> And she said, "Who would have declared to Abraham that Sarah would be suckling children? Yet I have borne a son in his old age."

21:8 "A child was usually weaned in its third year" (Westermann).

21:9 *mshq* Add *'im yiṣḥaq bᵉnāh* (LXX, 𝔘ᴹˢˢ).

21:10 "In E, Hagar is not Sarah's maid, but simply a household slave, who has become her master's concubine" (Skinner).

21:13 *lgwy* Insert *gādôl* (𝔐, LXX, 𝔖, 𝔘; cf. v. 18).

21:14   *śm 'l-škmh w't hyld*   Read *w't hyld śm 'l-škmh* (cf. LXX, 𝕾). "Ishmael is a child in Gen. 21 whereas according to 17:25 he was about sixteen years old. A transmitter has made a rather clumsy attempt at harmonization by changing the object to *hyld* so as to gloss over Abraham lifting Hagar's child onto her shoulders" (Westermann).

21:16   *wtś' 't qlh wtbk*   Read *wayyiśśa' 'et qōlōh wayyēb°k* (LXX).

21:17   *ml'k 'lhym*   See note to 16:7.

BEER-SHEBA (VERSION 1: E)

21:22ff.   "Scholars are so far virtually unanimous that the text of Gen. 21:22-34 consists of two layers: A, vv. 22-24, 27, (31 or) 32; and B, vv. 25-26, 28-30, 31 (or 31-32)" (Westermann).

21:22   *wpykl śr ṣb'w*   Delete. "Clumsily brought in from 26:26" (Westermann).

21:23   *w'm h'rṣ*   Read *w'm 'am h'rṣ* (cj. Ehrlich: haplography).

BEER-SHEBA (VERSION 2: J)

21:32ff.   Omitted (from R, with E? and J):

> After they made the pact at Beer-sheba, Abimelech left with Phicol, the commander of his army, and they returned to the land of the Philistines. And Abraham planted a tamarisk in Beer-sheba and invoked the name of the Lord, the eternal God. And Abraham stayed in the land of the Philistines for many years.

THE BINDING OF ISAAC (E)

22:2   *yhyd*   "It is very doubtful whether the usual meaning of *yhyd* is 'only.' Here the word cannot have this meaning, because Isaac was not the only son of Abraham.... *yhyd*, which is a substantive, not an adjective, means here, and very probably everywhere, *darling*. Cf. Judges 11:34..." (Ehrlich). LXX correctly renders *yhyd* as *agapēton*.

22:6,8   *'š*   "What is evidently meant here is equipment for producing fire, other than the wood itself, which is separately specified: Akkadian uses analogously *(aban) išāti*, 'fire (stone)'" (Speiser).

22:11   *ml'k yhwh*   Read *ml'k 'elōhîm* (𝕾) and see note to 16:7. It seems that some editor substituted "the Lord" for "God," which is used throughout the rest of the story. But see Westermann ad loc.

22:13   *ḥr* Read *'eḥād* (ca. 40 MSS, ᴍ, LXX, 𝕾, 𝕿ᴶ).

22:14b   I have omitted this half-verse, which may be a later addition:

> . . . as it is said to this day, "On the mountain of the Lord it is pro-
> vided."

22:15-18 Omitted (later addition):

> And the angel of the Lord [*ml'k yhwh*] called to Abraham a second
> time from the sky and said, " 'I swear,' says the Lord, 'that because
> you have done this, and have not withheld your son, your darling,
> I will greatly bless you, and I will greatly multiply your descen-
> dants so that they are as many as the stars in the sky and the sands
> on the seashore. And your descendants will seize the gates of their
> enemies, and in your descendants all the nations of the earth will
> be blessed, because you have obeyed my command.' "

22:23   *wbtw'l yld 't rbqh* Delete: gloss.

THE CAVE OF MACHPELAH (P)

23:1   *wyhyw* Insert *š^enê* (cf. 47:9, 28).

       šny ḥyy śrh Delete (>LXX, 𝕭).

23:15,16 The price that Ephron names (literally, "four hundred shekels of silver") is very high. "One sees how high the sum of 400 shekels is when
one compares it with the 17 shekels that Jeremiah pays for a field (Jer.
32:7) and the 6000 that Omri pays for the whole area on which
Samaria is to be built (1 Kings 16:24)" (Westermann).

23:16   *ksp 'br [lsḥr]* I have followed Ehrlich's interpretation.

23:20   Omitted:

> So the land and its cave passed to Abraham as a burial site, with
> the consent of the Hittites.

THE BETROTHAL OF REBECCA (LATE SOURCE)

24:1   In order to make it clear that this is a deathbed scene, I have inserted
"when the time of his death drew near" from 47:29. " 'Put your hand
under my thigh' occurs again only in 47:29 — another death-bed
scene! It is, in fact, only the immanence of death that can account for
the action here: had Abraham expected to live, a simple command
would have sufficed. . . . It is impossible to escape the impression that
in vv. 1-9 Abraham is very near his end, and that in 62-67 his death is

presupposed. It follows that the account of the event in JE must have occurred in this chapter, and been suppressed by the Redactor in favour of that of P (25:7-11), according to which Abraham survived the marriage of Isaac by some 35 years (cf. 25:20). The only question is whether it happened before or after the departure of his servant" (Skinner).

24:7   *'lhy hšmym*   Delete: gloss (>1 MS).

          ml'kw   Instead of leaving this word untranslated as at 16:7ff. and 21:17ff., I have translated it here as "presence."

24:15   *'šr yldh lbtw'l bn mlkh 'št nḥwr*   Read *'šr yāldâ mlkh 'št nḥwr* (cj. Dillmann) or *'šr yldh l'nāhôr*. "According to 29:5 Laban is the son of Nahor; according to 24:48 Rebekah is the daughter of Nahor. Bethuel plays no part in the story; it is likely that he is a subsequent insertion into 24:15, 24, 44 in anticipation of the P genealogy in 25:20 and 28:2, 5" (Westermann).

24:16   *yd'h*   Point *yād'â* (Ehrlich).

24:22   *msqlw*   Insert *wayyāśem 'al 'apāh* (ш; cf. v. 47).

24:24   *bt-btw'l 'nky bn-mlkh 'šr yldh lnḥwr*   Read *bat-nāhôr 'ānōkî*.

24:27   *'ḥy*   Point *'ᵃḥî* (LXX, ₵; cf. v. 48).

24:32   *wyb'*   Point *wayyābē'* (₪).

24:35   *m'd wygdl*   Read *wygdl m'd* (₷).

24:47   *bt-btw'l bn-nḥwr 'šr yldh-lw mlkh*   Read *bat nāhôr 'ānōkî*.

24:50   *wbtw'l wy'mrw*   Read *wy'mr*. "*wbtw'l* is obviously an addition in v. 50; the father could not be mentioned after the son, and in v. 53 only the mother is mentioned" (Westermann).

24:64   *wtpl*   "This does not mean 'she dismounted,' as people usually translate it, following LXX. This translation is mistaken, because no woman can dismount from a camel, especially when the animal is moving, as it is here. Onkelos gave the correct translation: she leaned down; cf. 6:4 and 14:10, and also the expression *npl l'pyw 'rṣh*, which frequently means nothing more than to bow deeply. Isaac had already come fairly near, and so that he might not hear what she said, Rebecca leaned from her high seat on the camel down to the slave who was walking beside it, in order to whisper the question to him" (Ehrlich).

24:67a   *śrh 'mw*   Delete.

24:67b   'mw Read *môt 'ābîw* (cj. Wellhausen, BHS). "It is striking that there has also been an insertion in v. 67a, *śrh 'mw*. Apart from the two additions Sarah does not appear in chapter 24. Looking back over the story, the reference could only be to the father who, at the beginning of the chapter, felt that he was near death" (Westermann).

THE DEATH OF ABRAHAM; ISHMAEL'S DESCENDANTS (P)
25:10   *qbr 'brhm wśrh* Read *qābar 'brhm śrh* (cj. Ehrlich).
25:11b, 18 These verses are generally attributed to J.
25:17   Insert after v. 12.

JACOB AND ESAU (J)
25:19-20 Omitted (from P):

>   And these are the descendants of Isaac, Abraham's son. Abraham fathered Isaac. And Isaac was forty years old when he took as his wife Rebecca, the daughter of Bethuel the Aramean of Paddan-aram, the sister of Laban the Aramean.

25:22-23 Omitted (later addition):

>   And the children fought inside her womb; and she said, "If it is like this, why do I live?" [adding *hyh*, with 𝔖] And she went to consult the Lord's oracle. And the Lord said to her, "Two nations are in your womb, / two peoples inside your body [deleting *yprdw*]. / But one shall be stronger than the other, / and the elder shall serve the younger."

25:25   'św Sarna mentions the possible connection with Arabic *gh-š-w*, "to cover, envelop," first proposed by Israel Eitan in *A Contribution to Biblical Lexicography*, New York, 1924 pp. 57f.

25:26b   Omitted (from P):

>   And Isaac was sixty years old when they were born.

25:30b   Omitted (later addition):

>   That is why he was called Edom, *Red*.

WIFE AND SISTER (VERSION 3: LATE SOURCE)
26:2b   Omitted (later addition):

>   "... stay in the land that I will show you."

26:3b-5 Omitted (later addition):

"... and I will give all these lands to you and to your descendants, and I will keep the solemn promise that I made to Abraham your father. And I will multiply your descendants like the stars in the sky, and will give them all these lands, and in your descendants all the nations of the earth will be blessed—all because Abraham obeyed me and kept my charge: my commandments, my laws, and my teachings."

ISAAC AND ABIMELECH; BEER-SHEBA (VERSION 3: LATE SOURCE)

26:12   *š'rym* Point *š*^e*'ōrîm* (LXX, 𝕊). "*m'h š'rym* cannot mean a hundredfold. First, it cannot be demonstrated that *š'r*, either in the O. T. or in the Mishna or anywhere else, has the meaning given in the dictionaries, of 'value' or 'measure'; and second, the noun after *m'h* would have to be in the singular (cf. 17:17, 33:19, Judg. 7:19, and 2 Kings 4:43). Also, a hundredfold harvest, especially in time of a general famine, is too enormous, even as an exaggeration. Finally, if that were so, *wybrkhw yhwh* would have had to precede this clause. According to the present succession of the two clauses, the content of the first can have nothing directly to do with the blessing of YHVH. For *š'rym* LXX and Peshitta correctly read *š*^e*'ōrîm* but misunderstood *m'h*. After this numeral the name of some measure, e. g., *s'h*, must be added; cf. Ruth 3:15, where what is measured is likewise barley. Perhaps especially with barley, which was considered as the commonest of all grains, it was usual to omit a more precise definition of measure. *mṣ'* does not mean *to reap*—and how could the word come to have this meaning?—but *to procure*. Even as rare and as expensive as the grain was in that year, Isaac procured a hundred measures of barley for sowing. How the harvest turned out is told to us in the indefinite *wybrkhw yhwh*" (Ehrlich).

26:15   Insert after v. 17.

26:16   "*'ṣmt mmnw*, in which the preposition corresponds to the *mn 'lby'n* of the Arabs, is literally = you are strong, as far as we are taken into consideration, i. e., you are stronger than is agreeable to us. Cf. Ex. 1:9, which doesn't mean 'more numerous and more powerful than we,' since that couldn't be true, but rather means 'more numerous and more powerful than is agreeable to us'" (Ehrlich).

26:18 *bymy* Read *'abdê* (𝔐, LXX, 𝔙).

26:22 *wprynw* Read *wprṣnw* (cj. Ehrlich).

26:24-25 Omitted (later addition):

> And the Lord appeared to him that night and said, "I am the God of Abraham your father. Don't be afraid, for I am with you, and I will bless you and multiply your descendants for the sake of my servant Abraham." And he built an altar there, and invoked the Lord's name.

26:34-35 From P; insert before 27:46.

ESAU CHEATED OF THE BLESSING (WHY JACOB WAS SENT TO LABAN, ACCORDING TO J)

27:5 *lhby'* Read *lᵉ'ābîw* (LXX).

27:7 *lpny yhwy* Delete. "The doubled *lpny* at the end of v. 7, stylistically extremely harsh, speaks against all explanations, and such a literary lapse can scarcely be attributed to the narrator of chapter 27. Moreover, the phrase 'bless in the presence of Yahweh' occurs only in this passage" (Westermann).

27:15 *ḥmdwt 'šr 'th bbyt* Delete. "*ḥmdwt*, which dangles in the air, is a later addition to explain how it happened that Esau's clothes were at Rebecca's disposal, as if they were his best clothes and not for everyday use. But in a biblical story no such explanation is required. The word in question belongs exclusively to hagiographic prose and is therefore too late for this story. The following clause as well seems to me suspicious" (Ehrlich).

27:23 *wybrkhw* Delete.

27:29aα Omitted (later addition):

> "May many peoples serve you / and many nations bow before you."

27:29aβ "brother . . . mother's son" Literally, "brothers . . . mother's sons." "The blessing is partly natural (²⁷ᵇ·²⁸), partly political (²⁹), and deals, of course, not with the personal history of Jacob, but with the future greatness of Israel. . . . [In 29aβ] the mention of *brethren* (pl.) shows that the immediate situation is forgotten" (Skinner).

27:30 *wyhy k'šr klh yṣḥq lbrk 't y'qb* Delete: doublet.

27:33 *mkl* Read *'ākōl* (cj. Kautzsch-Socin, BHS).

27:36   Omitted (later addition):

> And he said, "Is he named Jacob, *He Cheats,* so that he could cheat me twice? First he took my birthright, and now he has taken my blessing."

27:40b   Omitted (later addition):

> "... but one day you shall free yourself, and you shall break his yoke from your neck."

> "This verse is clearly prose and is an addition from a time in which Edom had freed itself from Judah, thus after ca. 840" (Gunkel).

27:45   *'d šwb 'p 'ḥyk* Delete: doublet of 44b.

WHY JACOB WAS SENT TO LABAN (ACCORDING TO P)

27:46   *mbnwt ḥt k'lh* Delete: gloss (>LXX).

JACOB AT BETH-EL (ACCORDING TO J)

28:10-11aα   I have used these verses at the beginning of both versions, since one version lacks an introduction; and I have used 19a at the end of both. The J version would thus include vv. 10, 11aα, 13-15a, 16, and 19; the E version vv. 10-12, 17-18, 20-21a, 22, and 19a.

28:13b-14   Omitted (later addition):

> "The ground which you are lying on I will give to you and to your descendants. And your descendants will be as numberless as the dust of the earth, and you will spread out to the west and to the east, to the north and to the south. And in you all the families of the earth will be blessed, and in your descendants."

28:15b   Omitted (later addition):

> "... for I will not leave you until I have done what [LXX: everything] I promised you."

JACOB AT BETH-EL (ACCORDING TO E)

28:21b   Omitted (from J):

> ... then the Lord will be my God ...

JACOB AND RACHEL, AND LEAH (J)

29:3   *h'drym* Read *hārō'im* (ᴍ, LXX^MSS, ᴀ).

29:8   *h'drym* Read *hārō'im* (ᴍ, LXX).

< NOTES >

29:24 Omitted (out of place; probably from P):
      And Laban gave his maid Zilpah to her, to his daughter Leah, as her maid.

29:27 *wntnh* Read *we'ettēn* (ᴍ, LXX, $, ℭᴾ, 𝔅).

29:28 *wy's y'qb kn* "Cf. 42:20; hardly 'he did so,' because what is expected in this context is some form of direct reply rather than long-term compliance alone" (Speiser).

29:29 Omitted (out of place; probably from P):
      And Laban gave to his daughter Rachel his maid Bilhah, to her as her maid.

29:30 *gm-'t* Read *'t* (LXX, 𝔅).

THE BIRTH OF JACOB'S CHILDREN (J)

29:31ff. "One can distinguish in chapters 29-30 an older from a later layer: the older is a narrative of the rivalry between Leah and Rachel in several acts, the later gives an account of the twelve children of Jacob in the form of a genealogy with the giving of names. . . . The narrative has two parts, 29:31-32 with 30:1-6 and 30:14-16 (18) with vv. 22-24 in an earlier form. . . . A later writer, using the system of the twelve that was available, has expanded it to a (secondary) genealogy in the course of which he has taken the reasons for the names from different sources and partly reshaped them" (Westermann).

29:33-35 Omitted (later addition):
      And she conceived again and gave birth to a son; and she said, "Because the Lord heard that I was unloved, he has given me this one also." So she named him Simeon, *He Has Heard.* And she conceived again and gave birth to a son; and she said, "This time my husband will be close to me, because I have borne him three sons." So she [reading *qār'â*, with ᴍ, LXXᴸ, $] named him Levi, *He Will Be Close.* And she conceived again and gave birth to a son; and she said, "Now I will praise the Lord." So she named him Judah, *Let Him Praise.* Then she stopped bearing children.

30:2 *wyḥr 'p* I have followed Ehrlich's interpretation.

30:7-13 Omitted (later addition):
      And Bilhah conceived again and bore Jacob another son. And

Rachel said, "I have played a huge trick on my sister, and it has suc-
ceeded." So she named him Naphtali, *Trickery*. And when Leah
found that she had stopped bearing children, she took her maid
Zilpah and gave her to Jacob as a concubine. And Zilpah bore
Jacob a son. And Leah said, "How lucky I am." So she named him
Gad, *Luck*. And Zilpah bore Jacob a second son. And Leah said,
"How fortunate I am: all the women will call me fortunate." So she
named him Asher, *Good Fortune*.

30:15   *lh* Read *lē'â* (LXX).

30:17   *wyšmʿ 'lhym 'l l'h wthr* Read *wthr l'h*.

      ḥmyšy Delete: later addition.

30:18   *śpḥty* Read *la'āḥôtî* (cj. Ehrlich). "I suspect that the text is not in order
here, not only because of this incongruity [that the explanation of the
name Issachar does not fit with the preceding story], but also because
of the consideration that when a wife gives her slave to her husband
as a concubine, this is not in itself praiseworthy and in the case of
Rachel is actually a self-seeking action. Such an action cannot, however, be highly valued by any god, much less by the God of the Hebrew
Bible. It is very likely that *la'āḥôtî* is to be read for *lšpḥty*. . . . The relative clause = 'for what I gave my sister for my husband'; in other
words, for giving her the mandrakes. Leah had given these plants,
which were believed to awaken and strengthen sexual desire, to her
childless rival to give to their husband. . . . Poor Rachel expected a
great deal from this remedy. A husband who has two wives and as
many concubines can very easily become debilitated; after eating the
mandrakes, however, the prospects of conception are increased by
vigorous and repeated embraces. Understood in this way, the action
which Leah is speaking about here is an action of self-denial, which
indeed deserves God's reward" (Ehrlich).

30:19-21   Omitted (later addition):

      And Leah conceived again and bore Jacob a sixth son. And she
said, "God has granted me a precious gift; now my husband will
treasure me, because I have borne him six sons." So she named him
Zebulun, *He Will Treasure*. And afterward she gave birth to a
daughter and named her Dinah.

30:22   *wyšmʿ ʾlyh ʾlhym* Delete: doublet of 22a.

30:24   Omitted (later addition):

> . . . saying, "May the Lord add to me another son."

This half-verse provides a second etiology for the name Joseph (as *May He Add*), and uses *yhwh* instead of *elohim.* "It is probable that this second meaning of *ywsp* or *ysp* is a later addition originating from someone who did not think that this name can come from *ʾsp*; cf. 1 Sam. 15:6, Micah 4:6, and Ps. 104:29. The verse in question can be identified as an interpolation through *lʾmr*, which introduces none of the other etiologies in this chapter" (Ehrlich).

JACOB OUTWITS LABAN (J)

30:32   *ʾbr* Read *ʾabōr* (אֶעֱבֹר).

30:32aβ   Omitted (later addition):

> . . . all the dark-colored ones among the sheep and all the spotted and speckled ones among the goats . . .

"Jacob will now pick out the unusually colored animals from the flock so that the flock which he has undertaken to care for contains only the normally colored. . . . The addition in v. 32, like that in v. 33, distinguishes between sheep and goats. . . . It is the same distinction as added by the glossator in vv. 35 and 40; it is the gloss of a specialist who expands the content correctly, namely, that the unusually colored among the goats (mainly dark or dark brown) and the sheep (mainly white) must be different" (Westermann).

30:33bβ   Omitted (later addition):

> . . . or if any of my sheep are not dark-colored . . .

30:35aβ   Omitted (later addition):

> . . . and all the speckled and spotted she-goats — every one with white on it — and all the dark-colored sheep . . .

"The glossator . . . wants to explain that the unusual coloring must necessarily be different in the case of the sheep and the goats. Before this he inserts *ʾt htyšym* = he-goats, with which he obviously wants to expand *ʿzym* = (she-) goats, a further sign of his concern for accuracy. The neutral *śh* would have stood originally in the narrative" (Westermann).

30:37aβ, bβ Omitted (later addition):

> . . . and of almond and plane-tree . . . exposing the white of the
> twigs . . .

30:38   *bšqtwt hmym* Delete: gloss.

30:38bα,γ Omitted (later addition):

> . . . where the goats came to drink . . . since they mated when they
> came to drink . . .

30:40   Omitted (later addition):

> But Jacob kept the sheep separate, and made them face the
> streaked and the dark-colored animals in Laban's flocks. So he
> bred flocks for himself which he didn't add to Laban's flocks.

JACOB'S FLIGHT (E?)

Westermann attributes this story to J. But the expansive style seems to me
more typical of E, as is the use of a dream as a vehicle of revelation. In addition,
the account of the speckled and streaked lambs and kids is different from J's
account in 30:32-39.

31:1,2   Transpose (Westermann).

31:3   Omitted (from J):

> And the Lord said to Jacob, "Return to the land of your fathers,
> where you were born, and I will be with you."

31:5b   Omitted (later addition):

> But the God of my father has been with me.

31:9   Omitted (later addition):

> Thus God has taken away your father's livestock and given it to me.

31:10-13 The omitted portion of this corrupt text (10, 12a), along with v. 11,
         reads as follows (in Westermann's reconstructed order):

> "Once, at the mating season, the angel of God [*ml'k 'lhym*] came to
> me in a dream and said, 'Jacob.' And I said, 'Yes.' And he said 'Look
> now and see that all the he-goats mounting the flock are streaked,
> speckled, and mottled.' And I looked and saw in the dream that
> the he-goats mounting the flock were streaked, speckled, and mot-
> tled."

31:12b   Insert after 13a (Westermann).

31:13   *h'l* Insert *hannir'eh 'ēlékā b^e* (LXX, 𝕿^{JP}).

31:18aβ,b Omitted (from P):

> . . . and all the possessions that he had acquired, the livestock in his

possession that he had acquired in Paddan-aram, to go to his father
Isaac in the land of Canaan.

31:20 Omitted (later addition):

And Jacob lulled the heart of Laban the Aramean by not telling
him that he intended to flee.

31:24 Omitted (later addition):

And God appeared to Laban the Aramean in a dream by night
and said to him, "Be careful to say nothing to Jacob, either good or
bad."

31:25 Omitted (later addition):

And Laban overtook Jacob. Now Jacob had pitched his tent on
Mount [Mizpah?], and Laban had pitched his tent [MT: kins-
men] on Mount Gilead.

31:26 *śyt* Read *'āśîtî l^ekā* ($).

wtgnb 't lbby Delete. "The history of the text shows that the words
wtgnb 't lbby are an addition (as in v. 20). They are missing in the
Greek, which has v. 27a instead; Syriac has *śyty* for *śyt*. Syriac has the
original text, which was altered by the insertion, because it did not
fit properly in front of the latter" (Westermann).

31:29 Omitted (later addition):

"It is in my power to do you harm; but the God of your father
spoke to me last night and said, 'Be careful to say nothing to Jacob,
either good or bad.'"

31:34b Delete (>LXX).

31:35 *wyḥpś* Insert *lābān b^ekol-hā'ōhel* (LXX).

31:39 *l' hb'ty 'lyk* "This = I did not *report* to you; cf. Lev. 13:2, Josh. 18:6, and
especially 2 Sam. 14:10" (Ehrlich).

31:39b Omitted:

. . . you claimed it from me, whether it was snatched by day or by
night.

31:42aβ Omitted (later addition):

". . . the God of Abraham and the *pḥd* [Fear? Awesome One?
Protection?] of Isaac . . ."

31:42b Omitted (later addition):

"But God saw my distress and my labour, and he gave his judgment last night."

31:44   *w'th* Insert *na⁽ᵃⁱśeh gal* (cj. Olshausen).

31:45   Omitted (later addition):

> And Jacob took a stone and set it up as a pillar.

31:46   *y'qb* Read *lābān* (𝕴).

         wyqḥw Read *wayyilqᵉṭû* (LXX).

31:46b–47 Omitted (later addition):

> . . . and they ate there on the heap. And Laban called it Yegar-sahadutha, *The Mound of Witness* [Aramaic], but Jacob called it Gal-ēd, *The Mound of Witness* [Hebrew].

31:48b–49aα Omitted (later addition):

> That is why it is called Gal-ēd, *The Mound of Witness*, and Mizpah, *Watch Post*, because he said . . .

31:49   *yhwh* Read *ᵉlōhîm* (LXX).

31:51–53a Omitted (later addition):

> And Laban said to Jacob, "Here is this mound, and here is this pillar that I have set up between you and me. This mound will be a witness and this pillar will be a witness that I will not pass beyond this mound to you and that you will not pass beyond this mound and this pillar to me, to do harm. May the God of Abraham and the God of Nahor judge between us, [gloss: the God of their father]."

JACOB PREPARES TO MEET ESAU (J)

32:4   *śdh 'dwm* Delete: gloss.

32:8b–9 Omitted (later addition):

> And he divided the people that were with him, and the sheep and the oxen [and the camels], into two companies [*maḥanot*]: he thought, "If Esau attacks one company, then the other may escape."

32:10–11 Omitted (later addition); I have retained *wy'mr y'qb 'lhy 'b[t]y* to introduce the prayer:

> "God of my father Abraham and God of my father Isaac, Lord, who said to me, 'Return to the land where you were born, and I will make you prosper,' I am not worthy of all the kindness that you have faithfully shown me. With nothing but my staff I crossed this river [*hyrdn hzh*]; and now I have grown into two companies."

32:13   Omitted (later addition):

"Yet you said, 'I will make you prosper and will make your descendants like the sands of the sea, so many that they cannot be numbered.'"

32:21   *y'qb*   Insert *bā'* (ɯ, LXX, 𝕿, 𝕿ᴶ).

32:22   *bmḥnh*   Read *bammaḥᵃnāyim* (cj. Ehrlich); *mḥnh* in this chapter means a group of people, not a place of encampment.

32:24   *'šr-lw*   Read *kol-'ᵃšer-lô* (ɯ, LXX, 𝕊, 𝕭).

JACOB WRESTLES WITH GOD AND BECOMES ISRAEL (ACCORDING TO J)

32:25   *'yš*   As in chapters 18 and 19, this means "(supernatural) being," who here turns out to be YHVH.

32:29   *w'm 'nšym*   Delete. This phrase, which has no relation to J's explanation of the name Yisra-El, seems to have been added by a scandalized editor, to weaken the assertion of a victory over God.

32:31   *pny'l*   Read *pᵉnûēl* (ɯ, Σ, 𝕊, 𝕭).

32:33   Omitted (later addition):
That is why to this day the children of Israel don't eat the thigh muscle that is on the socket of the hip, because Jacob's was wrenched at the thigh muscle.

THE MEETING OF JACOB AND ESAU (J)

33:2   *'ḥrnym w't*   Read *'aḥᵃrêhem w't* (LXX, 𝕊).

33:4   *wybkw*   Read *wayyēbᵉk* (dittography).

33:11   *hb't*   Read *hēbē'tî* (ɯ, LXX, 𝕊, 𝕭).

THE RAPE OF DINAH (EARLY SOURCE)

34:1ff.   "The origin of chapter 34 is to be sought in three different settings: (A) The family narrative, which is a self-contained and finished piece, can have originated toward the end of the patriarchal period. . . . (B) An account of the peaceful settlement of an Israelite group in the region of a Canaanite city can come from the period of the occupation of the land precisely because it has been reworked in accordance with Deut. 7. . . . (C) The author of the narrative as a whole presupposes Deut. 7 and is close to the language of P" (Westermann; see his detailed analysis of the evidence).
I have isolated the original (A) version of this story, which is quite

< NOTES >

bloodthirsty enough, and included the final version (C) as Appendix 3. (The old, independent poem of chapter 49, known as "The Testament of Jacob" — see Appendix 1 — seems to be referring to the A version's relatively tame murder of Shechem when it says, of Simeon and Levi, "For in their fury they killed a man.")

Omitted verses from the B version:

(9-12) "... and make a marriage alliance with us: give us your daughters and take our daughters for yourselves. And live among us, settle in our land, move around freely in it, and acquire property." And Shechem said to his father and brothers, "Do me this favor, and I will pay whatever you ask. Name as high a bride-price as you want and I will pay it. Just give me the girl as my wife." (15-18) "Only on one condition will we consent: if every male among you is circumcised as we are. Then we will give you our daughters, and we will take your daughters for ourselves, and we will live with you and become one people. But if you don't agree to be circumcised, we will take our sister [MT: daughter] and go." And their request seemed fair to Hamor and Hamor's son Shechem. (20-24) And Hamor and his son Shechem went to the city council and said to the men of the city, "These men have come to us in peace. Let them settle in our land and move around freely in it: the land is large enough to include them. We will take their daughters as wives and give them our daughters. But the men will consent to live with us and become one people only on this condition: that every male among us be circumcised, as they are. Won't their cattle, their possessions, and all their animals be advantageous for us? Let us agree to their terms, so that they will settle among us." And all the able-bodied men of the city agreed with Hamor and his son Shechem, and every male in the city was circumcised [LXX: on the flesh of his foreskin]. (27-29) The sons of Jacob attacked the ailing men [reading haḥōlîm] and plundered the city, because their sister had been violated. They took their sheep, their oxen, their donkeys, everything inside the city and outside it, all their wealth; and they took all their children and women as slaves [MT: and plundered everything in the house].

Omitted verses by the editor of the C version:

(7) . . . because he had committed an outrage in Israel by sleeping with Jacob's daughter, a thing not to be done. (13) . . . and they spoke deceitfully, because he had violated their sister Dinah . . . (25) . . . and killed every male. (26) . . . Hamor and his son . . . (30) . . . the Canaanites and the Perizzites.

34:6   Transfer after v. 7.

34:19   There is a phrase or a verse missing in the A version; I have inserted "and he had himself and his men circumcised" here and have added "and his men" in v. 26.

THE RETURN TO BETH-EL (R)

35:5   Omitted:

> And they departed. And a great terror fell on the cities all around, and none of them pursued the sons of Jacob.

This verse belongs after 34:31, in the B version of chapter 34.

35:6   *hw' b't-'l* Delete: gloss.

35:7   *'l b't-'l* Read *b't-'l* (LXX, 𝕾, 𝔘).

35:8   Westermann attributes this verse to J.

JACOB BECOMES ISRAEL (ACCORDING TO P)

35:9b–10 I have inserted these verses after v. 12.

35:10   *šmk y'qb* Delete (>LXX).

35:11   *wyqr' 't-šmw yśr'l* Delete (>LXX).

35:13   *bmqwm 'šr-dbr 'tw* Delete: dittography from v. 14 (>𝔘).

35:14f.   These verses were written or reworked by R.

THE DEATH OF RACHEL (J?)

35:19   *hw' byt lḥm* Delete: gloss.

GENEALOGIES (P)

36:1   *hw' 'dwm* Delete: gloss.

36:2   *bt-ṣb'wn* Read *ben-ṣb'wn* (𝔪, LXX, 𝕾); also in v. 14.
       ḥḥwy Read *haḥōrî* (cf. v. 20).

36:6   *'l-'rṣ* Insert *śē'îr* (𝕾).

36:19   *hw' 'dwm* Delete: gloss.

36:39   *hdr* Read *hᵃdad* (ca. 40 MSS, 1 Chron 1:50, ᴍ, ᴣ).

             bt my zhb Read *ben my zhb* (LXX, ᴣ).

36:40   *ytt* Read *yeter* (LXX^MSS; cf. v. 26).

36:43   *hw' 'śb 'by 'dwm* Delete: gloss.

JOSEPH AND HIS BROTHERS (EARLY SOURCE)

37:1ff.   Unlike the rest of Genesis, the Joseph story seems to be a unified whole (except for the variants and chapters 38 and 49). See Westermann, vol. 3, pp. 18ff.

37:1   I have used this verse, from P, as an introduction to the story of Judah and Tamar.

37:2   Omitted (from P):

        These are the descendants of Jacob. When Joseph was seventeen years old, he used to tend the flocks with his brothers (he was an assistant to the sons of his father's wives Bilhah and Zilpah), and he brought a bad report about them to their father.

    "The report that Joseph brought to Jacob did not concern all the brothers but only the four sons of Jacob's secondary wives. This then has nothing to do with the hatred of the brothers in vv. 3-11. . . . The narrative breaks off here" (Westermann).

37:3   *wyśr'l* See Westermann's discussion of the name "Israel" in the Joseph story (vol. 3, p. 119). For the sake of clarity, I have used "Jacob" throughout.

            ktnt psym The wonderful translation "coat of many colors" comes to us from the Septuagint via the Vulgate, the Luther Bible, and the King James version. Most modern scholars translate this phrase as "long-sleeved robe" or "ornamented tunic." But the great Koehler-Baumgartner Lexicon lists, along with "tunic reaching to ankles (?)," the alternative definition of "tunic of pieces of various colors (?)." Whether or not the robe was many-colored, it was a magnificent gift, as we know from 2 Samuel 13:18: "She was wearing a *ketónet passím*, for this is what unmarried princesses used to wear in earlier times."

37:4   *mkl-'hyw* Read *mkl-bānāyw* (ℭ, 5 MSS, ᴍ, LXX).

37:5   *wywspw 'wd śn' 'tw* Delete (>LXX).

37:8   *'l-ḥlmtyw w'l-dbryw* Delete: gloss.

37:10   *wyspr 'l-'byw w'l-'ḥyw* Delete (>LXX).

37:14bα Omitted (later addition):

> So he sent him out of the valley of Hebron ...

37:15-17 Omitted (later addition):

> A certain man met him as he was wandering in the fields. And the man said, "What are you looking for?" And he said, "I am looking for my brothers. Can you tell me where they are?" And the man said, "They have moved on from here. I heard them say they were going to Dothan." So Joseph went after his brothers, and he found them in Dothan.

37:21-22 Omitted (variant):

> And when Reuben heard this, he tried to save him from them and said, "Let us not take his life." And Reuben said to them, "Don't shed his blood; throw him into this pit in the wilderness, but don't lay a hand on him"—because he wanted to save him from them and restore him to his father.

37:23   *'t-ktnt hpsym 'šr 'lyw* Delete: gloss.

37:27   *'ḥynw* Delete: gloss.

37:28aα Omitted (variant):

> Then some Midianite traders passed by ...

37:29-30 Omitted (variant):

> And when Reuben returned to the pit, he saw that Joseph was not in the pit, and he tore his clothes. And he returned to his brothers and said, "The boy is gone! And I — how can I go home?"

37:32   Omitted (variant):

> And they sent the coat of many colors ...

37:35b   Omitted (doublet of 34b):

> Thus Joseph's father lamented for him.

37:36   Omitted (variant):

> And the Midianites sold him in Egypt to Potiphar, a courtier of Pharaoh's and captain of the guard.

JUDAH AND TAMAR (EARLY SOURCE)

38:1ff.   I have inserted this chapter after 37:1. "The narrative of Judah and Tamar has not been inserted into the Joseph story; it has nothing to

do with it but rather is an insertion into the Jacob story" (Westermann).

38:3   *wyqr'* Read *wattiqrā'* (12 MSS, 𝔐, 𝕋ᴶ).

38:5   *whyh* Read *wᵉhî'* (LXX).

38:8   "When a man's brother dies, the surviving brother is obliged to beget
children from his sister-in-law, the first-born of whom is regarded as
the child of the deceased" (Gunkel); cf. Deut. 25:5-10.

38:11   *šby ... wtšb* Point *šūbî ... wattāšāb* (Ball).

38:14   *wtks* Read *wattitkas* (𝔐, 𝔖, 𝕋).

38:17   *'šlḥ* Insert *lāk* (LXX, 𝔏, 𝔙).

        ttn Insert *lî* (𝕋ᴾ, 𝔖).

38:18   "The items named by Tamar were not chosen for their intrinsic value
but for purposes of personal identification. . . . The cylinder seal . . .
served as the religious and legal surrogate for the person who wore it,
and its impression on a document signalized the wearer's readiness to
accept all consequences in the event of non-compliance. . . . The pos-
sessor of such a seal was thereby marked as a responsible person; and,
as Herodotus reminds us, no Babylonian of any standing would ever
be seen without one. . . . All cylinder seals were perforated vertically
for suspension, so that the seal and the cord or chain on which it was
worn became a unit" (Speiser).

38:21   *mqmh* Read *hammāqôm* (𝔐, LXX, 𝔖, 𝕋ᴾ).

38:29f.   *wyqr'* Read *wattiqrā'* (3 MSS, 𝔐, 𝔖, 𝕋ᴶ).

        "Gen. 38 does not mention that the son of Tamar, born from the
event narrated here, is one of David's forefathers (but cf. Ruth 4);
it is important, however, from the overall context of the story
reported in the Old Testament" (Westermann).

JOSEPH AND HIS BROTHERS (CONTINUED)

39:1bα   Omitted (later addition):
        . . . Potiphar, a courtier of Pharaoh's and captain of the guard . . .

39:1bβ   *'šr hwrdhw šmh* Delete: gloss.

39:2b   *wyhy* Delete (>𝔖).

39:10   *lhywt 'mh* Delete: gloss (>LXX¹⁰⁶, 𝔈).

39:14   *'yš* Read *'īšî* (cj. Ehrlich).

39:20 *mqwm 'šr-'swry hmlk 'swrym* Delete: gloss.

39:21-23 Omitted (variant):

> But the Lord was with him and was faithful to him and won him the favor of the chief jailer. And the chief jailer put Joseph in charge of all the prisoners who were there, and everything that was done there was done through him. And the chief jailer didn't concern himself any further with what was in Joseph's charge, because the Lord was with him and brought success to everything he did.

40:1 Omitted (variant; I have retained the first three words):

> Some time later, the butler of the king of Egypt and the baker gave offense to their master, the king of Egypt.

40:5 Omitted (later addition):

> And both of them had dreams, each in the same night, each dream with its own interpretation — the butler and the baker of the king of Egypt, who were being held in the prison.

40:19 *m'lyk* Delete: gloss (>2 MSS, 𝔙).

41:8 *'wtm* Read *'ôtô* (LXX; cf. v. 8bα and v. 15).

41:9 *'t* Read *'el* (𝔪, LXX).

41:10 *'ty* Read *'ōtām* (𝔪, 𝕿ᴾ).

41:26 *ḥlwm 'ḥd hw'* Delete.

41:27 *ḥrqwt* Read *haddaqqôt* (LXX, 𝕾, 𝕿, 𝕿ᴶ).

41:34b Omitted (later addition):

> . . . and take one-fifth of the produce of the land of Egypt in the seven years of abundance.

41:35 *yd-pr'h* Insert *wᵉyitnû* (cf. v. 48).

41:40 *yšq* Point *yāšōq* or read *yaqšēb* (LXX). I have combined vv. 40 and 41.

41:45 *wyṣ' ywsp 'l-'rṣ mṣrym* Delete: scribal error? (>LXX).

41:46a Omitted (from P):

> Joseph was thirty years old when he entered the service of Pharaoh, king of Egypt.

41:54b Omitted (later addition):

> And there was famine in all lands; only in the land of Egypt was there food.

41:56 *'šr bhm* Read *kol-'ōṣrôt bār* (LXX?; cf. 𝔪, 𝕾).

     wyšbr Point *wayyašbēr* (𝔪ᴹˢˢ).

41:57a   *hʾrṣ*   Read *hāʾᵃrāṣôt* (ɯ, LXX).

42:1b   Omitted (fragment):

> . . . Jacob said to his sons, "Why do you stand looking at one another?"

42:5   Omitted (displaced from after 41:57?):

> And the sons of Israel came to buy grain among those who came, for there was famine in the land of Canaan.

42:6   *hwʾ hšlyṭ ʿl-hʾrṣ*   Delete: gloss.

42:8   Omitted (later addition):

> And Joseph recognized his brothers, but they didn't recognize him.

42:20   *wyʿśw kn*   Delete: gloss.

42:22   Omitted (variant):

> And Reuben spoke up and said to them, "Didn't I tell you not to sin against the boy? But you wouldn't listen, and now his blood must be accounted for."

42:24   *wydbr ʾlhm*   Delete (>LXX^MSS).

42:33   *wʾt*   Insert *šeber* (LXX, 𝔖, 𝕿^MS, 𝔙).

42:35   Omitted (later addition):

> And as they were emptying their bags, every man's money pouch was in his bag. And when they and their father saw the money pouches, they were afraid.

42:37   Omitted (variant):

> And Reuben said to his father, "Kill my two sons, if I don't bring him back to you. Put him in my care, and I will bring him to you again."

43:17b   *hʾyš*   Delete (>LXX, 𝔖).

43:18   *wlhtnpl ʿlynw*   Delete: gloss.

43:26aβ   *hbyth*   Delete (>𝔙).

43:29   *ʾmrtm*   Insert *lᵉhābîʾ* (LXX).

44:1b   Omitted (later addition):

> . . . and put each one's money on top of his pack.

44:2aβ   Omitted (later addition):

> . . . along with his money for the grain.

44:4   *ṭwbh*   Insert *wᵉlāmmâ gᵉnabtem lî ʾet-gᵉbîᵃ hakkesep* (LXX; cf. 𝔖, 𝔙).

44:5 "...the [cup] he drinks from and looks into to see what lies hidden": "Divination by means of liquids is well attested, especially in Mesopotamia.... Oil or water was poured into a bowl or cup, and omens were then based on the appearance of the liquids inside the container...." (Speiser).

44:8 *ksp* Read *hakkesep* (ωι, LXX, 𝕊, 𝕋, 𝕋ᴶ).

44:21 *w'śymh 'yny 'lyw* For the meaning "to look upon with benevolence, take care of," cf. Jer. 24:6, 39:12, 40:4.

45:2 *mṣrym* Read *kol-hammiṣrîm* (LXX).

   wyšm' byt pr'h Delete: gloss.

45:7b Omitted (later addition):

   ...to preserve you as a remnant in the land, and to save your lives in a great deliverance.

45:8 I have followed Westermann in reversing the order of 8a and 8b.

45:21 *wy'św-kn bny yśr'l* Delete: gloss.

45:24b Omitted:

   And he said to them, "Don't be troubled [literally: tremble (with rage, excitement, agitation)] on the way."

   Either the text is in disorder or Joseph's intention here is obscure because of a failure of style — unlikely for a writer of such wonderful clarity.

46:1-50:26 "The Joseph narrative as far as chapter 45 runs its course in a continuous, coherent, and clearly arranged sequence of events; the conclusion, chapters 46-50, is complicated. It contains expansions, doublings, breaks in continuity, and much that does not seem to belong immediately to the Joseph narrative" (Westermann). I have followed Westermann's exegesis and concluded the Joseph story with the following passages: 46:5b, 28-34, 47:1-6, 11-12, 27a, 29-31, 48:1-2, 8-9, 10b-12, and 50:1-10a, 14. In addition, because an account of Jacob's death is missing, I have added the following verses from the P version: 49:1a, 28bβ, and 33 (modified to fit the context). The rest of these final chapters I have relegated to Appendix 1; they include passages by P and by a number of independent (mostly late) sources.

GENEALOGIES (P)

46:13 *wywb* Read *w'yāšûb* (Num. 26:24, 1 Chron 7:1, ωι, LXX).

46:21   *ḥy wr'š mpym wḥpym* Read *wa'ᵃḥîrām wᵉšûpām wᵉḥûpām* (Num. 26:38f.).

46:22   *yld* Read *yāldâ* (29 MSS, 𝔐, 𝔖, 𝔗).

JOSEPH AND HIS BROTHERS (CONTINUED)

46:28   *lhwrt lpnyw* Read *lᵉhiqqārôt lô* (LXX).

        gšnh Delete: gloss.

46:29   *wyr' 'lyw* Read *wayyar' ōtô* (cj. Westermann).

46:31   *w'l-byt 'byw* Delete: gloss (>LXX).

46:32   *ky-'nšy mqnh hyw* Delete: displaced from v. 34.

JOSEPH'S LAND POLICY (LATE SOURCE)

47:15,16   *ksp* Read *hakkesep* (𝔐, 𝔖, 𝔗).

47:16   *lkm* Insert *leḥem* (𝔐, LXX, 𝔗ᴶ).

47:21   *h'byr 'tw l'rym* Read *heᵉᵉbîd 'tw laᵉᵃbādîm* (𝔐, LXX, 𝔙).

47:24   *wl'kl ltpkm* Delete: gloss (>LXX).

47:26b Omitted (later addition):

        …the only land that doesn't belong to Pharaoh is the priests' land.

JOSEPH AND HIS BROTHERS (CONTINUED)

47:30   *bqbrtm* Read *biqbūrātî* (cj. BHS; cf. 50:5).

48:1   *'prym* Insert *wayyābō' 'el-yaᵉᵃqōb* (LXX).

48:12   *l'pyw* Read *lô 'apayim* (LXX, 𝔖).

JACOB BLESSES JOSEPH'S SONS (A LATER VERSION: LATE SOURCE)

48:20   *ybrk* Point *yᵉbōrak* (LXX, 𝔖).

THE TESTAMENT OF JACOB (EARLY SOURCE)

49:4   *'lh* Delete (>𝔙).

49:6a   Omitted (gloss):

        "Let my soul not come into their council, / nor my heart be joined
        with their assembly."

49:6b   *'qrw-šwr* The parallelism makes it very unlikely that this phrase refers
        to hamstringing an ox. Vawter (*Catholic Biblical Quarterly* 17 [1955], 4f.)
        notes that in Ugaritic "bull" often means "male" or "male dignitary" and
        that "the verb *'qr* has as its basal meaning 'upturn,' 'destroy,' 'render
        useless.'"

49:9   *bny* Read *bᵉgay* (cj. Westermann).

49:10   *šylh* Read *mōšlōh* (cj. Ball) or compare *šylh* with Akkadian *šēlu*, "ruler" (Nötscher, *Zeitschrift für die alttestamentliche Wissenschaft* 47 [1929], 323ff.). The reference in this verse is to the coming of the Davidic monarchy and its conquest of the Canaanite nations.

49:18   Omitted (gloss):

        I long for your deliverance, Lord.

49:19-20 *'qb: m'šr* Read *ᵃqēbām: 'šr* (LXX, 𝔖, 𝔙).

49:22   *bn prt* "This must mean a *bull*. Joseph is compared to a bull in Deut. 33:17 also. *prt* would then = *pārâ*, or a scribal miscopying of the latter. Accordingly, the name of some animal must lie hidden in *bnwt ṣᶜdh*. In Arabic *banāt ṣaᶜdat* is a name for the wild ass.... In *ᶜly šwr*, which obviously should correspond with the *ᶜly ᶜyn* of the parallel, *šwr* does not mean wall, but is the name of a place in the vicinity of which a steppe with a spring was located; cf. 16:7" (Ehrlich).

49:24b-25aα   Omitted (later addition):

        ...by the hands of the Mighty One of Jacob, / by the name [*miššēm*] of the Shepherd, the Rock of Israel, / by the God of your father, who helps you.

49:25aβ   *w't* Read *wᵉᶜēl* (3 MSS, 𝔪, LXX, 𝔖).

49:26   *'byk gbrw 'l-* Read *'ābîb wᵉgibᶜōl* (cj. de Vaux; thus Speiser). 26aα is obviously corrupt; this is the least unlikely of the emendations.

        hwry 'd- Read *harᵉrê 'ad* (LXX).

JACOB'S DEATH AND BURIAL (P)

49:28bβ   *'šr* Delete (>3 MSS, LXX, 𝔖).

49:29   *'my* Point *'ammay* (Gunkel, BHS; cf. v. 33).

49:30   *'t-hśdh* Delete: gloss.

49:32   Omitted (gloss):

        ...the property and the cave that is in it, bought from the Hittites.

49:33   Omitted (from R):

        ...when Jacob had finished giving his instructions to his sons...

JOSEPH AND HIS BROTHERS (CONTINUED)

50:3   *ky kn yml'w ymy hḥnṭym* Delete: gloss.

50:4   *dbrw-n'* Insert *'ālay* (LXX).

50:10   *yrdn* "Flowing water, as in Mandaean, with no reference to the Jordan" (Guillaume, *Promise and Fulfilment: Essays Presented to S. H. Hooke*, ed. F. F. Bruce, Edinburgh, 1963, p. 126). "'Jordan' is not a proper noun but seems to be an East Mediterranean word for river. Cf. Iardanos in *Odyssey* 3:291f., *Iliad* 7:135" (C. H. Gordon, *Before the Bible*, New York, 1962, pp. 284f.). *yrdn* certainly has this meaning in Job 40:23, where it refers to the cosmic river or to the Nile or to both; Ps. 114:3, where it is parallel to *ym* and refers to the parting of the Red Sea; and 32:11, where Jacob says, "With nothing but my staff I crossed this river (*hyrdn hzh*)," obviously referring to the Jabbok. The river is probably the river (or brook) of Egypt, which formed the border between Canaan and Egypt. "In other words, Joseph's followers performed the mourning ceremony at a Canaanite village just beyond the border" (Graves and Patai).

50:10b-11   Omitted (later addition):

> And he mourned for his father for seven days. And when the inhabitants of the land, the Canaanites, saw the mourning at Goren ha-Atad, they said, "This is a solemn mourning for the Egyptians." That is why it was called Abel-mitsrayim, *The Mourning of Egypt* (it is on the far side of the Jordan [or: the river]).

JACOB'S DEATH AND BURIAL (CONTINUED)

50:13   *'t-hśdh*   Delete: gloss.

JOSEPH AND HIS BROTHERS (CONTINUED)

50:14   *'ḥry qbrw 't-'byw*   Delete: gloss (> LXX).

EPILOGUE (VERSION 2: LATE SOURCE)

50:25   *mzh*   Insert *'itkem* (14 MSS, ɯ, LXX, 𝕾, 𝔙).

Acknowledgments

I would like to express my gratitude to Bill Moyers, for the invitation that led to this book; to Norman Lear, for his loving, generous heart; to Michael Katz, my agent, for his usual grace and expertise; to Hugh Van Dusen, my editor, for helping everything to happen in the right way; to David Bullen, for designing this and so many other beautiful books; to John Tarrant, for letting me pilfer some of his insights; to Chana Bloch, Elaine Pagels, and John Tarrant, for their invaluable criticism of the Introduction; and to Vicki, for more than words can say.

About the Author

Stephen Mitchell has become widely known for his original and definitive translations of spiritual writings and poetry. He was born in Brooklyn, New York, in 1943 and studied at Amherst, the University of Paris, and Yale. His previous books include *Dropping Ashes on the Buddha*, *The Selected Poetry of Rainer Maria Rilke*, *The Book of Job*, *Tao Te Ching*, and *The Gospel According to Jesus*. He lives with his wife, Vicki Chang, an acupuncturist and healer, in Sonoma, California.